teachers
meeting the challenge of change

Presented to Parliament by
the Secretary of State for Education and Employment
by Command of Her Majesty

December 1998

Cm 4164 £8.65

Contents

Foreword by the Prime Minister   4

Foreword by the Secretary of State for Education and Employment   5

Executive summary   6

Chapter 1   The imperative of modernisation   11

Chapter 2   Better leadership: pay, performance and development   21

Chapter 3   Better rewards for teaching   31

Chapter 4   Better training   43

Chapter 5   Better support and new possibilities   55

Chapter 6   Conclusion   65

Annex A   Teacher recruitment measures of October 1998   71

Foreword

I have always said that education is this Government's top priority. The teaching profession is critical to our mission. First-rate teachers and headteachers are indispensable to giving all our children the best possible start in life.

There are very many excellent teachers up and down the country. But we need more. We need to give them better support, leadership and recognition. We need excellence to become the norm. And we need a modern professional structure capable of achieving our goals.

These are urgent national imperatives. As teachers themselves are often the first to accept, they can only be met by radical change.

This Green Paper sets out the Government's proposals to improve the teaching profession. It addresses the critical issues of training, recruitment, leadership and support for teachers in the classroom and beyond. It also describes our proposals for pay and performance. We must reward good teaching better, recognising its vital role in raising standards.

This is a programme of investment for reform – significant extra resources in return for significant improvements in standards.

These proposals are for consultation. We are seeking your views and will be responsive to suggestions for improvement. But the status quo is not an option. After decades of drift, decisive action is required to raise teaching to the front rank of professions. Only by modernisation can we equip our nation for the new century. I hope you will join us in meeting the challenge.

> ...'the most fundamental reform of the teaching profession since state education began...'
>
> *Tony Blair*
> *September 1998*

Tony Blair
Prime Minister

Foreword

Our schools depend, above all, on the skill, commitment and dedication of our heads, teachers and support staff. Having taught for seven years in a further education college, I know what it is like. Sheer hard work, sometimes frustrating, but always rewarding when you see the difference you make to a young person's life.

The Government is committed to a substantial programme of investment in education – £19 billion extra over the next three years – because, like you, we want world-class schools for our children in the new century. In a world of rapid change, every pupil will need to be literate, numerate and prepared for the citizenship of tomorrow. They will need the self-esteem and confidence to learn throughout life, and to play an active part at work and in their community.

Part of this investment is for a new pay and rewards structure. As many teachers, heads and school governors would accept, the present arrangements reflect a different era. We need a new vision of a profession which offers better rewards and support in return for higher standards. Our aim is to strengthen school leadership, provide incentives for excellence, engender a strong culture of professional development, offer better support to teachers to focus on teaching in the classroom, and improve the image, morale and status of the profession.

Major reforms are already underway to raise standards, but we can only realise the full potential of our schools if we recruit and motivate teachers and other staff with the ambition, incentives, training and support to exploit this opportunity. That is why this Green Paper is so important.

I recognise that we are proposing a significant change for the profession, but I believe passionately that it is the right change For the first time in a generation, we have both the opportunity to change the profession's pay and rewards for the better and the investment to make it happen.

This Green Paper is about the future of the children you teach, the profession that you are committed to and the community which values you. Please read it and let us have your views.

David Blunkett
Secretary of State for Education and Employment

Executive summary

1 Chapter 1 sets out the case for modernising the teaching profession. Investment in technology, classroom support and school buildings is opening up new possibilities for raising standards and achievement across the board. This needs to be matched by a new vision of the teaching profession – with good leadership, incentives for excellence, a strong culture of professional development, and better support for teachers to focus on teaching – to improve the image and status of the profession.

2 Major reforms are already underway to raise standards. Sustained investment is available as a result of the Government's Comprehensive Spending Review to support them. But we can only realise the full potential of our education system if we attract and motivate teachers and other staff with the ambition, incentives, training and support to exploit this opportunity. That is why this Green Paper is so important.

3 The Government's goal is a world-class education system where every school is excellent or improving or both. The modernisation of the teaching profession is central to this ambition. Our reforms are based on the following objectives:

- to promote excellent school leadership by rewarding our leading professionals properly;

- to recruit, retain and motivate high quality classroom teachers, by paying them more; and

4 Chapter 2 explains our proposals for strengthening school leadership. Good heads are crucial to the success of schools. The best heads are a match for the best leaders anywhere. We need to develop strong leaders, reward them well and give them freedom to manage, without losing accountability.

5 We propose to extend the pay scale so that successful heads in tough jobs can earn higher salaries. We will allow fixed-term contracts to link rewards to the achievement of agreed objectives. We plan to strengthen performance-related pay for heads by providing trained outside support for governing bodies in appraising heads.

6 We also want to offer schools freedom to recognise leadership by other teachers who give strategic direction in schools. Some promising teachers may take parts of the headship qualification early as a fast-track to headship.

- to provide better support to all teachers, and to deploy teaching resources in a more flexible way.

In the process, we hope to create a new and positive culture of excellence and improvement within the profession, and to restore teaching to the status it deserves – a profession essential to our success in the next century.

7 High quality training for heads is essential to support strong leadership. Existing programmes have proved their worth and we propose to develop them into a national training framework for headship with three levels:

- qualification, through the national Professional Qualification for Headship which we propose should be mandatory by 2002 for all those coming new to headship;

- induction, to consolidate the skills of new heads; and

- extension, to refresh the skills of experienced heads.

8 A National College for School Leadership will provide a focus for leadership training, combining cutting-edge educational content with the best in public and private sector management.

9 Chapter 3 explains our proposals for a new pay system to reward teachers for high performance, and improve career prospects. We propose two pay ranges for classroom teachers, with a performance threshold at the end of the first range giving access to a new, second range for high performing teachers.

10 The key features of the new system would be:

- new appraisal arrangements involving a thorough annual assessment of performance against agreed targets;

- a pay scale leading up to the performance threshold;

- success at the performance threshold requiring high and sustained levels of competence, achievement and commitment; and

- higher pay ranges and new professional expectations for teachers above the threshold.

11 We plan to introduce a new School Performance Award Scheme to reward a significant number of schools each year. The scheme would reward staff as teams or individuals, including classroom assistants and other support staff.

12 We will provide training to help heads, teachers and governors operate the new system. We will set out clearly the roles and responsibilities of those involved, and arrangements for proper monitoring and accountability. We will continue our review of teachers' pensions to develop arrangements that better meet the needs of the education service, individual teachers and their employers.

13 Chapter 4 explains our plans to give teachers the training and support they need to do their jobs well and to progress in their careers.

14 We propose to make initial teacher training more flexible and more rigorous so that all new teachers have the skills to teach well, through:

- new national tests for all trainee teachers to guarantee high level skills in numeracy, literacy and Information and Communication Technology (ICT);

- new pre-course provision for trainee teachers;

- reviewing procedures for Qualified Teacher Status;

- developing a network of schools pioneering innovative practice in school-led teacher training;

- encouraging the widest possible range of applicants through more flexible training courses; and

- extending employment-based routes into teaching.

15 We also propose to introduce a new national fast-track scheme to attract able graduates and move outstanding teachers quickly through the profession. Fast-track teachers would receive additional training in return for accepting supplementary contracts with a longer working year and greater mobility.

16 Continuing commitment to professional development should be at the heart of teachers' careers. We propose to support this through:

- a contractual duty for all teachers to keep their skills up-to-date;

- a new focus on professional development bringing together national, school and individual priorities;

- a national Code of Practice for training providers and a new inspection programme to ensure that training gives value for money and delivers results;

- more training out of school hours to minimise disruption to children's education;

- a review of training arrangements for supply teachers; and

- continued emphasis on equipping teachers with good ICT skills.

17 Training is important for all who work in schools. We propose to pilot Individual Learning Accounts for all school staff and use National Vocational Qualifications to improve the training of teaching assistants. We will make it easier for teaching assistants, who want to do so, to train as teachers.

18 Chapter 5 explains our proposals for strengthening teaching and learning by using the full potential of teaching assistants and school support staff.

19 We will increase the number of teaching assistants by 20,000 full-time posts (or equivalent) by 2002. We will produce guidance on good practice to encourage teachers to use assistants effectively.

20 We are already working with schools to find ways of helping them streamline their administration. We are reviewing our own practices to reduce bureaucratic burdens on teachers and to communicate with them more effectively.

21 ICT opens up new ways of teaching and learning and we are investing in infrastructure and training to allow all schools to benefit. The National Grid for Learning provides links and signposts to websites such as the DfEE Standards Site which make information readily accessible.

22 It makes sense for schools to share resources and to encourage lifelong learning in their local communities. Small schools can benefit particularly from sharing resources. We propose to establish a Small School Support Fund to provide pilot funding to help small schools make this kind of investment.

23 We are determined that all school staff should have better working conditions. Annual capital investment in schools will more than double over the next three years. In addition, we will pay for projects to improve staff working environments and help teachers have access to the equipment they need to work effectively.

24 Chapter 6 invites everyone who is interested in young people's education to consider the proposals in our Green Paper. We want to see a national debate. We would welcome your views on:

- our aims for the profession – higher status, better prospects, a rewarding career structure, less bureaucracy, more freedom to focus on teaching, a new professionalism, greater individual accountability, more flexibility and higher standards;

- our proposed new structure for the teaching profession;

- a broadening of the leadership group with more pay and greater use of fixed-term contracts for tough headship jobs and effective performance-related pay;

- a prestigious National College for School Leadership and a new framework for headship training;

- appraisal of teachers' performance as the basis for professional judgements on pay and career development;

- a performance threshold giving access to higher pay for teachers with consistently strong performance;

- a School Performance Award Scheme to reward achievement by whole schools;

- more flexibility and more rigour in initial teacher training;

- systematic career and professional development;

- a national fast-track scheme to help talented trainees and teachers advance rapidly in the profession;

- more effective use of, and better training for, teaching assistants and other support staff; and

- a Small School Support fund to encourage small schools to work together.

The consultation ends on 31 March 1999.

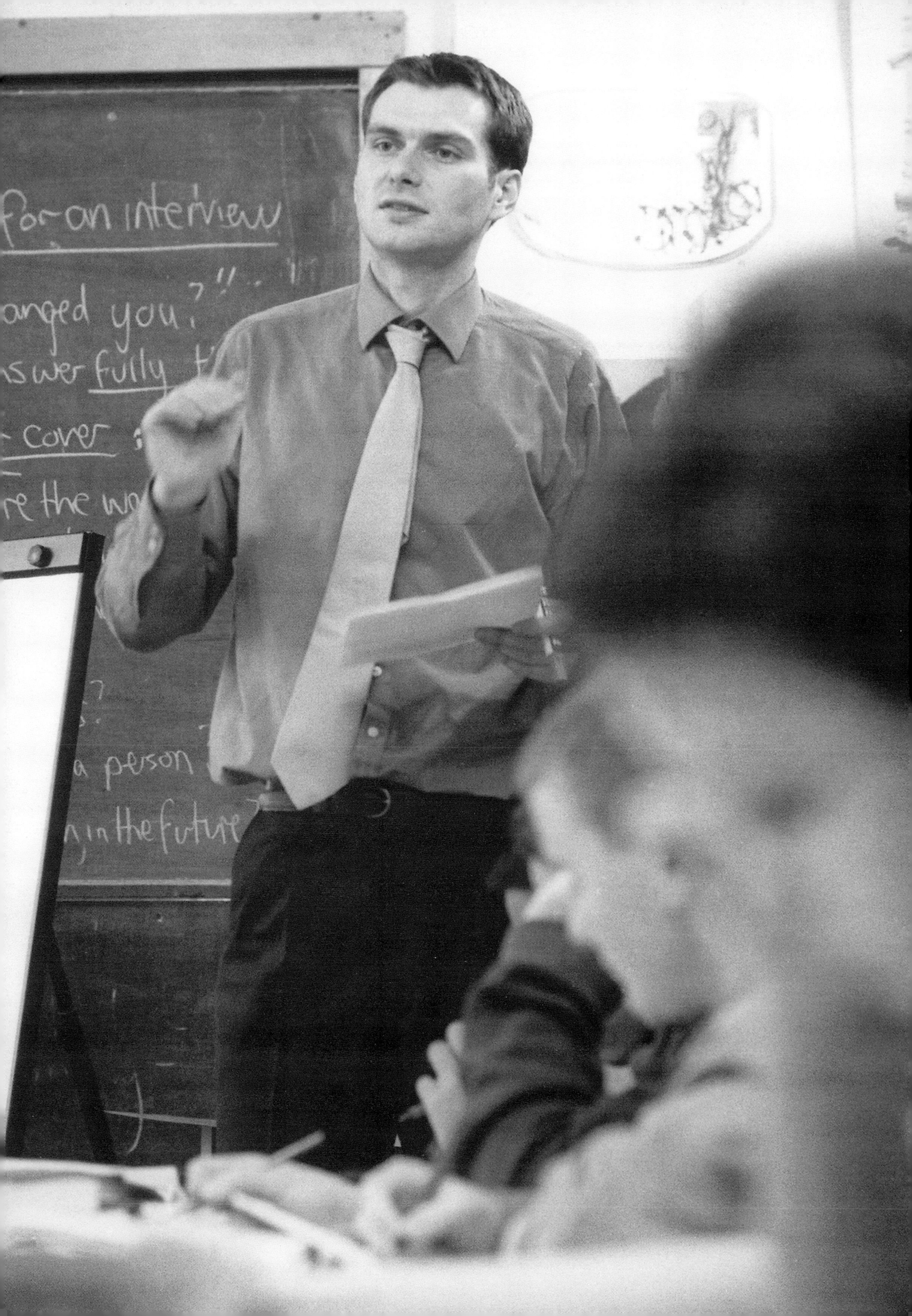
for an interview
a person
in the future

The imperative of modernisation

The Government wants a world-class education service for all our children. Major reforms are already underway to raise standards. They need to be matched by a new vision of the teaching profession. That is why this Green Paper is so important. We want to hear the views of everyone who is interested in young people's education. We propose a new staffing framework to support our objective: an education system which has high expectations of all children, which recognises, supports and rewards excellent teaching, which seeks constant improvement and achieves consistently high standards.

A world-class education service

1 The Government wants a world-class education service for all our children. Every pupil should become literate, numerate, well-informed, confident, capable of learning throughout life and able to play an active part in the workforce and the community. All pupils should have the opportunity to become creative, innovative and capable of leadership. Pupils will need education for a world of rapid change in which both flexible attitudes and enduring values have a part to play.

2 These words have often been part of the rhetoric of educational debate. The challenge in the next decade is to make them a reality. An enormous amount of good work has gone on in the education service over many years – often against the odds – to raise standards and to open up equality of opportunity for all children. We need to go further. This means continuing to raise standards for all; it also means encouraging learning to high levels among those who, even in the recent past, have left school with little or no benefit from eleven years of compulsory education. Achieving this ambitious goal requires a new vision of education for the 21st century which is shared by government, parents, school governors, teachers, other school staff, Local Education Authorities, teacher trainers, employers and by society as a whole. None of these partners can succeed alone. Together we can create an education service second to none.

3 At the heart of this vision is the school which takes responsibility for improving itself and which challenges and works with every pupil to reach ever higher standards. The school of the future, working in partnership with parents and the community, will often be a centre of lifelong learning. It will offer pupils excellent teaching in the basics and a wide range of learning opportunities, some provided at the school site and others elsewhere. It will be outward looking, constantly seeking to learn from other good schools, drawing on libraries and other sources of learning and examining the evidence of what works. It will be well-led and managed, reward good performance and it will offer pay, conditions and training for all its staff that reflect the central importance of education to society. Above all it will seek continuous improvement, expect change and promote innovation.

4 Government support means that a new opportunity is now there for the taking. The extra £19 billion the Government is investing in education over the next 3 years will mean an average 6 per cent increase in local authority education provision in each of the next 3 years, a substantial increase in the Standards Fund and a doubling of annual investment in schools capital by the end of the Parliament. The Government's major investments in Information and Communication Technology and teaching assistants will make possible effective new combinations of staff and technology to raise standards and extend learning opportunities. All schools, including those in the most disadvantaged circumstances, can take up the challenge of raising standards. We will recognise and provide support for schools facing economic and social disadvantage, but this cannot be allowed to be an excuse for under-performance. Just as radical change has proved possible in many other sectors in the last decade, so it can be achieved in education in the next decade.

Changes in the classroom

5 These developments will have profound implications for teachers individually and for the profession as a whole. At the heart of what teachers do will remain the good, well-taught lesson – which has proved its effectiveness. But many new possibilities are emerging. Throughout this century teachers have had to choose between prioritising the needs of large groups or following up the diverse needs of individuals. Now for the first time they can realistically do both.

6 New technology can add new dimensions to lessons, improving both effectiveness and presentation. Already innovative schools in the specialist schools network and elsewhere are challenging old assumptions and demonstrating what is possible. Diagnosis of pupils' strengths and weaknesses can be improved by new computer software. Information can be drawn from the world wide web by pupils and teachers alike. Pupils' capacity to undertake independent research is being dramatically enhanced. Pupils' homes can be networked to schools. Teachers, through interactive technology, will be able to teach their traditional lessons to pupils not just in one location but several. New technologies are giving pupils with special educational needs improved access to learning. None of this is wishful thinking: it is already beginning to happen.

7 In the end, however, it is the quality of teaching and the support available to teachers which will make the difference. The increasing numbers of teaching assistants and support professionals in schools will change approaches to teaching and learning. With trained assistants, teachers can choose between large groups and small ones, assigning additional staff to provide extra assistance to those with special educational needs or to help push on the gifted or those with particular talents. Other adults – full time or part time – can bring specialist skills or knowledge into the classroom.

8 Using specialist staff and new technology can help relieve teachers of the bureaucratic burden which, all too often, has distracted them from their core function of teaching children well. Electronic registers, assessment and recording systems, software for managing budgets, search facilities for computerised records, better use of bursars and administrative staff all have a part to play in freeing teachers to teach and improving the effectiveness of schools.

9 Furthermore, the doubling of Government investment in school buildings over the lifetime of the Parliament will transform our school buildings and provide modern facilities for pupils. It will provide teachers and other staff with the working conditions which other professionals have long taken for granted. The shabby staffroom and the battered electric kettle – which endured for so long because teachers always choose to put their pupils first – can become things of the past.

10 None of this is wishful thinking either: it is beginning to happen. The challenge is to make the best practice of some schools into the reality for every school.

> "Technology has revolutionalised the way we work and is now set to transform education. Children cannot be effective in tomorrow's world if they are trained in yesterday's skills. Nor should teachers be denied the tools that other professionals take for granted"
>
> *Tony Blair*
> *"Connecting the Learning Society" 1997*

A new professionalism

11 Schools will rise to the challenge of the future in many different ways. The Government has no wish to impose any single model. It wants to leave scope for discussion at local level about flexibility in the school year or in the way school premises are used. It does, though, want every school and teacher to have the opportunity to advance with confidence into the 21st century and make the most of new investment and technology to raise standards and achievement across the board.

12 In the future, teachers will find themselves extending traditional teaching through masterclasses, work with small groups or one-to-one sessions with pupils to review progress. As well as being teachers in the traditional sense, they will also become managers of learning, using all the human and technical resources available to help children achieve. Again this is not wishful thinking: it is already beginning to happen.

13 All this demands a new professionalism among teachers. The time has long gone when isolated, unaccountable professionals made curriculum and pedagogical decisions alone, without reference to the outside world. Teachers in a modern teaching profession need:

- to have high expectations of themselves and of all pupils;

- to accept accountability;

- to take personal and collective responsibility for improving their skills and subject knowledge;

- to seek to base decisions on evidence of what works in schools in this country and internationally;

- to work in partnership with other staff in schools;

- to welcome the contribution that parents, business and others outside a school can make to its success; and

- to anticipate change and promote innovation.

Modernising the teaching profession: why it is necessary

14 Teachers themselves would readily acknowledge that the present reality does not match this ambitious vision. The challenge of modernisation is immense. There are fundamental issues to tackle.

More good leaders

15 While there are many good and some outstanding headteachers, we need more. OFSTED estimates that one in six primary schools and one in ten secondary schools suffers from poor leadership. It is proving increasingly difficult to recruit enough primary heads in some areas. Yet strong leadership is essential if teachers are to do the best possible job in the classroom.

Attracting good teachers

16 Recruitment to teacher training has become increasingly difficult. The Government has already taken steps to tackle some of the immediate recruitment problems through financial incentives, on the job training and support for local recruitment strategies. (Details of the package announced on 27 October 1998 are at Annex A). But we are under no illusions about the scale of the longer-term challenge. Stated simply, the present reality of teaching too often compares unfavourably with the growing range of alternative careers for successful graduates. Although recruitment to primary teaching remains broadly on target, teaching still attracts too few entrants with excellent A level results or degrees. Only 14 per cent of entrants to initial teacher training for primary schools in 1996-97 were men.

17 Meanwhile recruiting sufficient teacher trainees for a growing number of secondary subjects – especially those where the competition from other sectors is most fierce – is difficult. There is a shortfall of 25 per cent on overall recruitment targets at secondary level with the most serious shortages in subjects such as mathematics, science, modern foreign languages and technology.

18 These problems at entry to teacher training are compounded by high wastage rates in the early years of teaching. Of every 100 students who start primary teacher training in 1999, we estimate that only 60 will start teaching in maintained nursery and primary schools the year they qualify and a further six a year later. The picture at secondary level is likely to be even worse. Of every 100 students we estimate that only 58 will start teaching in maintained secondary schools that year and a further six a year later.

19 These are disturbing statistics but perhaps not surprising. There are many good schools and good teachers and teaching has obvious intrinsic rewards but the profession as a whole does not attract enough ambitious young people or those in later life looking for a career change.

Few incentives for excellence

20 Good performance is not sufficiently rewarded. Although the present pay system allows for the award of extra pay for excellent performance, fewer than one per cent of teachers have ever benefited because such recognition is not part of the culture. Few professions have turned their back on linking pay and performance to the same extent as teaching. The tradition in teaching is to treat all teachers as if their performance was similar, even though in every staffroom teachers themselves know this is not true.

Unsystematic professional development

21 Opportunities for professional growth and development are inadequate. Teachers do not have systematic access to information about what schools at the cutting-edge are doing or about research and inspection findings. As a result too many teachers, through no fault of their own, are not aware of proven best practice. Until the advent of the literacy and numeracy strategies and the national headship training programmes, this was true even in those critically important areas.

Inadequate support

22 Meanwhile, workload studies by both the School Teachers' Review Body and the teacher unions suggest that teachers spend, on average, less than half their working time teaching face to face. Too much time is spent on administrative chores, some of which could be done better, and more cost-effectively, by others. In general, working conditions are below the standard which well-qualified graduates in other fields take for granted. The queue to use the ageing photocopier is an all too familiar sight in staffrooms across the country.

Poor image

23 No wonder teachers often complain that morale is low. The teaching profession as a whole has not, for many years, had the status among the general public which it deserves. Its public image has been further undermined by its defensive reaction to criticism of some aspects of the education service and of its performance compared to other countries. Teachers too often seem to be afraid of change and therefore to resist it. Teachers have too often felt isolated. Many seem to believe they are unique victims of the process of constant change, although the reality is that in many other sectors change has been more revolutionary and had greater impact on pay, conditions and styles of work.

24 Poorly managed change, conflict in the 1980s and early 1990s and uncertain funding for education over many years have also made their contribution to this state of affairs. Worst of all, there has been a widespread sense among many teachers and their leaders that nothing can be done to change it. The fatalistic view – which adds to the sense of despondency – seems to have been that it has to be this way.

25 Yet the evidence shows that teachers do make a real and positive difference. They can enable all pupils to succeed and ensure that the deprivation of one generation is not reinforced and passed on to the next. A visit to any one of thousands of successful schools in all parts of the country demonstrates that where there is good, positive leadership and a team of staff ready to take on the challenge of improvement, standards rise and teaching is highly rewarding. Indeed, one of the ironies of education today is the contrast between the negative impression of the profession as a whole and the sense of energy and purpose to be found in many individual schools.

26 The aim of the proposals set out in this Green Paper is to ensure that the culture of ambition and achievement which characterises the country's most successful schools becomes the culture of the entire profession.

Modernising the teaching profession: key to raising standards

27 We are working to develop a world-class education service. The standards agenda set out in *Excellence in schools* in July 1997 is now well on the way to implementation. It puts in place the conditions in which all schools can succeed. It gives them responsibility for improving themselves.

28 The Government recognises the importance to schools of external factors. The measures we are taking to reduce inequality, to overcome poverty and to provide a way out of economic and social deprivation are all part of a cross-cutting approach to improving the circumstances in which the most challenging teaching takes place.

29 We have already taken some significant steps to enhance the skills and status of teachers. Legislation to establish a General Teaching Council has already been put on the statute book. The Council will come into operation in 2000 and provide an independent voice for the teaching profession. We have introduced the new grade of Advanced Skills Teacher. We have strengthened initial teacher training. Through the Standards Fund, the Government is making a substantial investment in leadership training and providing the largest ever programme of investment in the skills of classroom teachers.

30 The Government's Comprehensive Spending Review has provided the sustained investment over the three year period 1999-2002 to ensure that these policies can be turned into reality. The Government now offers the necessary combination of the long term goals, the strategy and the investment to transform education in this country.

31 The potential is there to raise standards to levels never previously achieved. By early in the new century, we could have an education system which is the envy of the world. **But this will only be possible if we attract, retain and motivate sufficient teachers and other staff with the sense of ambition, the incentives, the training and the support to exploit this unprecedented opportunity**. That is why the programme set out in this Green Paper is so important. That is why the Government looks forward to debating it constructively with teachers, governors and parents in the months ahead, and that is why it is essential that we embark as soon as possible on a thorough-going modernisation of the teaching profession.

> "Teachers are our most precious asset. Up and down the country they are doing a job against the odds. In future they will be doing it with us and with our support"
>
> *David Blunkett,*
> *1 October 1998*

The new staffing framework

32 In order to achieve these ambitions, we propose a new staffing framework for schools. It recognises for the first time not only the different roles of the various staff in schools but also the relationships between them. It also acknowledges the contribution of teaching assistants, support staff and resources from outside the school.

33 Central to the staffing framework is a new career structure for teachers, which rewards teachers for high performance and offers incentives for success. We describe in the following chapters how this would work. New performance management arrangements based on annual appraisal, would underpin career and professional development and influence pay. Systematic and regular training and development would be available at every stage. The new structure would take teachers from their initial training, through induction and into a classroom teaching role in which there would be real prospects of salary progression and professional growth. A broader leadership group would encompass all teachers who provide strategic leadership in schools, including Advanced Skills Teachers as leaders of teaching and learning.

34 Our objectives in this modernisation process are clear. We intend:

- to develop an education system which achieves consistently high standards, has high expectations of all children whatever their background, seeks constant improvement and takes change in its stride;

- to recognise the key role of teachers in raising standards;

- to ensure we have excellent leadership in every school;

- to exploit the opportunities for new approaches to teaching and learning which extra staff and investment in Information and Communication Technology make possible;

- to provide rewards for success and incentives for excellence;

- to create a culture in which all staff benefit from good quality training and development throughout their careers so that they can adopt proven best practice, develop innovative ideas and manage constant change;

- to attract a sufficient supply of good teachers and a greater share of the able and talented; and

- to improve the esteem in which the teaching profession holds itself and is held by the community.

35 We will be accused of being visionary and excessively ambitious. We plead guilty. After the years of drift, vision and ambition are surely what is needed. Creating a world-class education service was never going to be easy but that is what the economy and society of the future require. A modern teaching profession is central to this process. If teachers rise to the challenge of modernisation in the next few months they themselves, along with pupils and parents, will undoubtedly be major beneficiaries. We urge all those with an interest in the future of our education system to give this Green Paper the most careful consideration and to grasp the historic opportunity that now presents itself.

Better leadership: pay, performance and development

Good heads are crucial to the success of schools. We need to develop strong leaders, reward them well and give them the freedom to manage, without losing accountability. We want to offer schools freedom to recognise leadership by other teachers who help the head give strategic direction in schools. Our key proposals for strengthening school leadership are:

On pay:

- more pay for tough jobs with the most successful heads earning up to £70,000;
- robust performance-related pay for heads and the option of fixed term contracts;
- support for governing bodies in appraising heads;
- a broader leadership group with a new contract; and
- the expansion of the Advanced Skills Teacher grade.

On career and professional development:

- a national framework for headship training for aspiring, new and existing heads;
- a fast-track to headship for the most promising teachers;
- a new National College for School Leadership; and
- better career planning for heads.

The role of the head

36 All the evidence shows that heads are the key to a school's success. All schools need a leader who creates a sense of purpose and direction, sets high expectations of staff and pupils, focuses on improving teaching and learning, monitors performance and motivates the staff to give of their best. The best heads are as good at leadership as the best leaders in any other sector, including business. The challenge is to create the rewards, training and support to attract, retain and develop many more heads of this calibre.

37 Our reform programme is taking further the delegation of funding and responsibility to schools. It is designed to attract talented leaders by giving them the freedom to manage and to allocate resources in accordance with school priorities. In return, all schools must be accountable. As we said in *Excellence in schools*, our goal is that every school should be excellent or improving or both. For schools demonstrating consistent success we will provide additional freedoms, including a new light touch inspection system. For those not performing as well as they should the new arrangements in the School Standards and Framework Act will ensure that they receive, as early as possible, the necessary challenge and support to set them on the road to improvement.

38 Headship is challenging and rewarding but it can also be isolating. Heads need to have close links with senior colleagues and with the chair of the governing body. They also need an outside perspective. Leadership training can provide this, as can involvement in local networks or schemes such as Partners in Leadership which is run by Business in the Community and the Teacher Training Agency. This outward-facing dimension will become increasingly important as schools open up their facilities and learn from each other.

"Schools will continue to face changing expectations, including the need to ensure higher standards of achievement, collect and analyse more data about children's achievement, offer a wider range of services, adapt educational provision to the needs of the local community and provide education in a range of settings. The rapidly-growing use of Information and Communication Technology is also creating new challenges for schools. It follows from all this that the future task of the headteacher is perhaps even more challenging than it is at present. .."

Ninth Report of the House of Commons Education and Employment Select Committee November 1998

Heads and governing bodies

39 Heads need good working relations with their governing body. Governing bodies are responsible in law for the overall conduct of their school and heads are accountable to them for the school's performance. It is important that each respects the other's role. Governing bodies need to give heads the freedom to manage. Heads need to give governing bodies the information they require to carry out their responsibilities effectively. New regulations following on from the Schools Standards and Framework Act will clarify the role of the governing body in setting the strategic direction of the school and the role of the head in developing policy, leading and managing within that overall strategy.

40 From September 2000, heads will have responsibility for implementing the new performance management and pay system proposed in this Green Paper. These new arrangements will need to be reflected in heads' contracts and in the performance management

Chapter 2: Better leadership: pay, performance and development

> **Rockingham Primary School, Corby**
>
> Rockingham Primary School has taken a lead in supporting community and parental involvement in school. The headteacher, Sue Cordwell, has worked to raise awareness of the importance of this work, which is included in the School Improvement Plan and supported from the school budget. The school established a community room which forms a focal point for Family Learning programmes and aims to create a welcoming atmosphere where parents and the wider community feel part of the school.
>
> Close links have been developed with the local Early Excellence Centre. The school developed a Family Literacy Project with the help of a small grant from the Basic Skills Agency and has continued to develop Family Literacy and Numeracy provision. Parents are now more likely to get involved in supporting reading and other school activities. Northamptonshire Local Education Authority regards the programme of parental and community involvement as a model of good practice.
>
> Sue Cordwell said "Forging links with the community and enabling parents and carers to establish a real place in our school has been a slow learning process but one that has given us great pleasure and which is making a significant difference to our whole community's learning, most especially for our children."

policy of the governing body. To help heads and governors we will provide model policies and, through the leadership programmes and the Standards Fund, ensure training is available to every school.

Rewarding the performance of heads

41 Pay arrangements for heads should reflect the importance of their leadership role and enable the most successful heads to earn more. We have already asked the School Teachers' Review Body to review the current arrangements to ensure that the salary of primary heads better reflects the work they do. Governing bodies need to consider how challenging headship posts are in deciding their exact place on the pay spine. In many cases a fixed term contract of, say, five years linked to the achievement of agreed objectives would be a good option. High salaries of up to £70,000 per year could be used to attract successful and experienced heads to schools which need leading out of special measures or serious weakness.

42 All heads are on performance-related pay, at least in theory. The evidence demonstrates that in practice this is not working properly. Governors and heads often feel uncomfortable with the arrangements. A 1998 study by the Centre for Economic Performance at the London School of Economics suggests that implementation is patchy, with fewer than two-thirds of heads in 1996/97 receiving the annual salary statement to which they are entitled.

43 Rewarding heads well for good performance is appropriate in its own right. It is also central to the development of a school culture which encourages and rewards excellence. Each year, heads and governing bodies should agree targets for school improvement against which the head's performance would be assessed and which should form the basis for decisions on performance-related pay. Pay enhancements should depend on clear evidence of progress in pupil attainment. Targets could also include broader indicators of school success such as better pupil attendance rates, employability of

school leavers or measurable impact of expanded community links.

44 New statutory arrangements for appraisal come into force from September 1999. We will set out proposals in a detailed document on performance management to be published early in 1999. We envisage that the responsibility should be on the governing body to ensure that the head's performance is properly appraised each year and to take account of the outcome in its review of the head's pay. However, governing bodies need access to high quality, independent advice for functions such as appraising the performance or deciding the remuneration of a head where they cannot properly rely on the advice of their own head.

45 In dealing with appraisal and performance pay for a head we believe that the governing body ought to make use of a suitably trained external adviser in order to ensure rigorous standards of assessment. The adviser would be involved in appraising the head's performance and providing advice on the setting of the head's annual targets and on performance pay. The Local Education Authority should provide advice and background information on comparative salaries to inform the governing body's pay decisions. It may be sensible for the assessor who monitors the operation of the school's overall performance pay policy as proposed in paragraph 87 also to act as the governing body's adviser on appraising the head.

Support for governing bodies

46 Local Education Authorities need to tailor their support to governing bodies effectively in line with the principle of intervention in inverse proportion to the success of the school. The new Code of Practice on Local Education Authority – School Relations sets out how authorities should use their formal powers to advise on the appointment of head or to raise concerns about the performance of a head. Authorities should also consider how to encourage the sharing of expertise across schools – for example by putting governing bodies in touch with experienced heads when they are involved in crucial but relatively infrequent decisions such as the appointment of a new head.

47 We will discuss with governors' representatives the support they need in developing their role. Governors' involvement in schools is vital. We want to avoid those who volunteer as governors being discouraged by demands on their time and expertise. We will particularly want to support them through training and by making available model policies and guidance to support the arrangements proposed in this Paper.

A broader leadership group

48 While heads are of crucial importance, leadership in schools is often shared and studies show that this shared leadership responsibility is a characteristic of successful heads. In many schools the members of senior management teams help heads give strategic direction in schools. We believe that governing bodies should have discretion to reflect this by appointing key senior staff to a new leadership pay spine subject to similar terms and conditions as those which currently apply to heads and deputies.

49 Governing bodies should have discretion over how many leadership positions to create in line with their own staffing structure and budgets. We would expect Advanced Skills Teachers to be included as leaders of teaching and learning. Secondary schools might also include members of the senior management team, heads of major departments, or those with important pastoral responsibility. At primary level, the leadership group may well not go wider than the head and any deputy or Advanced Skills Teacher, with possibly the heads of infant and junior departments at large schools. It is important that small schools do not create layers of bureaucracy which impede good teaching.

50 A single pay spine could cover all leadership posts, with the top points available only to heads. Governing bodies would decide a suitable pay range for each post on the basis of national guidance and advice from the head. Pay progression would be based on annual performance reviews against individual targets, including those relating to pupil performance and drawing on the outcomes of the annual appraisal process. Given the prospect of higher pay it is

---

Advanced Skills Teachers (ASTs)

Each AST is formally required to perform an outreach function and to spread good practice. How this is done is not prescribed centrally. Some valuable examples of innovative approaches have already been identified during the introductory phase. ASTs are already:

- developing and delivering in-service training;

- demonstrating good classroom practice both in person and through ICT links to other schools and teacher training institutions;

- designing and testing new teaching materials;

- giving masterclasses out of school hours;

- helping other teachers develop teaching styles based on high expectations; and

- improving continuity and progression between the primary and secondary phases.

ASTs are a particularly valuable resource for schools in need of excellent teachers to turn them round, but which experience problems recruiting staff of the right calibre.

right to expect additional commitment in return. Those on the leadership pay spine would not be covered by the restrictions on working time in the teachers' contract.

51 We envisage that Advanced Skills Teachers (ASTs) would also form part of the leadership group. The AST grade was created in 1998 to provide a career path for excellent teachers who want to remain classroom practitioners and who pass a rigorous assessment against national standards. The pay scale for ASTs extends up to £40,000 per year, with progression subject to regular performance reviews.

52 ASTs spend most of their time in the classroom, but also have a new contractual duty to support and to advise other teachers. The AST grade is now being introduced in specialist schools and in Education Action Zones. One hundred ASTs are expected to be in post by the end of 1998. The number is planned to expand to 5,000 by the year 2000 reaching a total of 10,000 in the longer term.

Career development for leaders

53 The evidence points strongly to the importance of heads of departments and curriculum leaders in driving improvements in teaching and learning. We believe that schools should recognise their importance in allocating training budgets. Introductory leadership and management courses from the headship training programme should be available to teachers who are taking on management responsibilities for the first time, whether or not they intend ultimately to aim for headship. Successful teachers can also gain – and contribute – valuable experience working on a part-time or seconded basis in the advisory services of Local Education Authorities.

54 We want to encourage faster promotion to headship for the most able. We intend to introduce a fast-track to headship to let promising teachers take modules of the headship qualification early. This would be open to any teachers who were identified in appraisal as promising candidates. It would not be confined to those on the new fast-track route described in paragraphs 116-119, although we hope fast-track teachers would develop as rapidly in mid-career as in their first years in the profession.

Leadership development

Unilever recognises that leadership is a crucial factor in the success of a school and that the job of school management is an increasingly demanding one requiring high level skills and determination. Much business management expertise and experience is directly relevant to the needs of schools.

Unilever is encouraging its group companies to provide occasional placements for heads and other senior school managers to help develop their management skills. It also provides training programmes based on business practice.

Unilever is working in partnership with seven schools in Tower Hamlets which are particularly interested in improving school management. The heads and deputies are identifying and meeting personal development needs based on Unilever's competencies and processes. Each prepares a personal development plan which is supported by access to company training programmes and appropriate external courses, and by mentoring support.

Headship training programme

55 In a rapidly changing world, schools cannot stand still. Nor can their heads. That is why we propose to invest up to £100 million in headship training over the next three years. Training should be fresh and relevant, practical and professional. We have laid the groundwork through three schemes:

- the National Professional Qualification for Headship (NPQH) for aspiring heads has been designed and is in the early stages of implementation;

- the HEADLAMP Programme for heads in their first two years in post has become established;

- the Leadership Programme for Serving Heads has been trialled and began in November 1998.

56 We intend to develop this valuable early work into a national training framework for headship and ensure that all heads have access to high quality training at every stage of their careers. The new programme will have 3 levels:

Headship Training Framework

Qualification

through the National Professional Qualification for Headship;

– *as the benchmark for entry to headship*

Induction Programme

building on the existing HEADLAMP programme

– *to consolidate and reinforce the skills of new heads*

Extension Programme

building on the serving heads programme

– *to give experienced, successful heads the opportunity to stretch their skills*

National Professional Qualification for Headship

Gillian Metcalfe, Deputy Headteacher at Newsome High School and Sports College, Huddersfield hoped that the NPQH would be a bridge between the practice and theory of headship.

"The life of a deputy is full to overflowing and it is quite easy to feel that the NPQH is another burden or a series of hoops to jump through in order to get a headship. What I obtained from training and development was, to a large part, dependent on what I contributed to the activities.

The networking among candidates was invaluable and I shall keep in touch with many of them. We had a common approach to training and assessment. It was obvious that we were all willing to learn, and were eager to try out new found approaches and then discuss how they had worked out in practice. The training sharpened our minds on the key issues of headship and allowed us to try out strategies in a supportive environment alongside other senior managers."

Gillian Metcalfe has now completed a range of activities which have emerged as a direct result of the NPQH, including:

- a thorough premises analysis;

- review of procedures for monitoring and evaluating of teaching and learning across the school;

- regular staff performance coaching; and

- a different, more strategic approach to devising the School Development Plan.

57 We intend that the National Professional Qualification for Headship should be mandatory by 2002 for all those coming new to headship. We will work with the Teacher Training Agency to strengthen the qualification further in the light of evaluation. Each stage of headship training should build on the one before and reinforce skills and experience already acquired. At all three stages successful heads should play a leading role in designing and delivering training to ensure that the focus is firmly on the practical skills of school leadership.

58 Experienced heads have much expertise to share with their colleagues. They also need to refresh their skills and to gain new inspiration. Research indicates that heads are most effective between three and seven years into the post, suggesting that without a fresh perspective there is a risk of the pressures of the task wearing them down. Over 1,200 have registered for the serving heads programme this year and from April 1999 we will enable over 3,000 heads a year to benefit. We will ensure that every head on the programme is paired with a senior leader from local business or industry so that they can learn from each other and develop new opportunities, including secondments, sabbaticals, further links with industry and advanced training. All of this will help heads remain at the cutting edge of their profession.

A National College for School Leadership

59 To underline our commitment to improving the quality of school leadership, we will establish a prestigious new National College for School Leadership. The college will combine high quality educational content with the best in public and private sector management. It will have close links with leading business schools. It will have a prestigious site commensurate with its importance, with the highest quality ICT facilities. It will also have a virtual presence on the National Grid for Learning so that all leaders and aspiring leaders can take advantage of its resources. We will issue a prospectus for the college early in 1999 and intend it to be in operation by September 2000.

60 The main function of the college will be to provide a national location for residential courses relating to all three headship programmes. It will also work with the network of regional leadership centres which we expect to continue to deliver leadership training. University links could enable it

---

Leadership Programme for Serving Heads

OFSTED's recent inspection characterised Ermine Junior School, Lincolnshire as an improving school. Following the Leadership Programme for Serving Heads, headteacher Stephen Hopkins now feels well-equipped to continue this improvement. "The programme was sharply focused around diagnostic feedback from members of my staff, using questionnaires based on models of leadership and management which have had proven success in commercial and public sector organisations across the globe. Feedback on my leadership qualities, in relation to the characteristics displayed by highly effective headteachers, and the range of leadership styles I currently use has given me a reliable basis upon which to set targets for my continuing professional development."

Stephen Hopkins believes that his role as a mentor for members of his Senior Management Team has also benefited. The Senior Management Team is now drawing on his experience as a framework to guide their own work.

to be an awarding body for educational academic qualifications. It could also award Associate, Fellowship or – exceptionally – Companion status to heads at different stages of development. The College will provide a focus for school leaders to meet their peers from different regions in the UK and internationally. It will provide sabbaticals for talented serving heads and will commission research activity across industry and education relevant to raising standards in schools. It could also offer advice on potential career paths so that heads have a clear sense of options.

Career paths for heads

61 Some heads will choose to move to a more challenging headship role in a different school, perhaps one in need of rapid improvement. Our pay proposals are designed to reward those who take on such challenges. We are also keen to see other opportunities develop, particularly at primary level. We set out in paragraphs 158-162 our intention to support projects for small schools to work more closely together. These experiments might involve federations of small schools with a single head – which could make high quality leadership skills more widely available and offer new career paths for those talented primary teachers who have reached headship relatively early in their career.

62 For experienced heads who want different challenges we will encourage their skills to be used elsewhere in education. There are well-established links between headship and advisory or inspectoral work in Local Education Authorities. We believe there is a strong case, given the newly defined role of Local Education Authorities, for chief education officers to be recruited from among heads. We will ensure that the new National College for School Leadership links up with innovative Local Education Authorities and the Virtual Staff College for senior education officers to develop training programmes to prepare heads for leadership in Local Education Authorities.

63 Headship is demanding. For those who want a less pressurised role before retirement new stepping down arrangements give flexibility for heads and teachers with responsibilities to change jobs within teaching towards the end of their careers while protecting their pension entitlements. Some 500 such heads and teachers have taken advantage of the new arrangements since September 1997. We will also work with the relevant unions to develop guidelines for counselling to back up these arrangements and show how heads and senior teachers can be helped in practical ways to adapt to a different role.

Tackling underperformance by heads

64 OFSTED findings imply that up to one in seven of our schools is not well led. This is too many. We do not disguise the fact that this may mean uncomfortable choices. Where a head is unable to provide satisfactory leadership then evidently action needs to be taken. If a school is clearly failing then powers exist to close the school if necessary and install new leadership. In some cases competency procedings may be appropriate. We want to ensure that where it is in the best interests of the head and school to part company this is done at the right time and in the right way. We propose to put additional resources into the School Improvement Grant within the Standards Fund with the express purpose of making it easier for underperforming schools to get the strong leadership they need. We will publish further details in due course.

3

Better rewards for teaching

A modern pay system should attract and retain sufficient people of the right calibre, reward good performance, improve career progression and enable the best teachers to gain high rewards. It should offer a great deal of flexibility for schools within a national framework. It should offer a significant rise in salary after some five to seven years for high performing teachers with a track record of consistently strong performance who are successfully assessed at a performance threshold and who are prepared to meet higher professional expectations.

Key proposals are:

- higher pay for good teachers with assessment at a new performance threshold leading to a new upper pay range;
- more rigorous annual appraisal arrangements to influence decisions on the pay of individual teachers at all levels;
- a new School Performance Award Scheme;
- more systematic performance management in schools; and
- clear accountability and monitoring of the new system.

65 Teachers deserve rewards for good performance, better career prospects, opportunities to keep their skills and subject knowledge up-to-date and the support and working environment to do their job. We propose two pay ranges for classroom teachers, with a performance threshold giving access to a new, higher range for high performing teachers with a track record of consistently strong performance. Crossing this threshold would be a significant career step. Above the threshold, teachers would continue to focus on classroom teaching but would be expected to take responsibility for making a wider contribution to raising standards in their school.

The objectives of a new pay policy

66 A national framework covers the pay and conditions of some 500,000 teachers in England and Wales. Each year, the School Teachers' Review Body (STRB), on the basis of a remit given to it by the Secretary of State for Education and Employment, consults the teacher organisations, government and employers and then offers advice on levels of pay, the pay structure and the conditions of service of teachers. The outcomes are then laid down annually in the Pay and Conditions Document which has statutory force.

67 The current pay and conditions arrangements for teachers suffer from significant problems. While in theory they allow for excellence to be recognised in salary terms, in practice good classroom performance is not sufficiently rewarded. The excellence points allowed for in the present scheme have been awarded to fewer than one per cent of all teachers. Instead, teachers move up a pay spine almost exclusively on the basis of time served, regardless of performance, up to a maximum of nine points which are worth £22,410 at December 1998 rates. Beyond that, progression depends in practice on taking on additional responsibility outside the classroom.

68 As a result, the majority of teachers are clustered around a limited range of points on the teachers' pay spine which they reach relatively early in their career. About a third of primary teachers are on a salary point of £22,410 with a further third receiving up to £3,000 more to reflect additional responsibilities. There are small numbers on higher salaries. In secondary schools a fifth of teachers are on a salary point of £22,410 with a further half receiving up to £7,000 more to reflect additional responsibilities. Prior to the introduction in September 1998 of the Advanced Skills Teachers Scheme, the only real way for successful, ambitious teachers to earn more was to take on a management role.

69 The main reason why the system has rewarded experience and responsibility but not performance is cultural. Heads and teachers have been more reluctant than comparable professional groups to distinguish the performance of some teachers from others, except through the award of responsibility points. The tradition, to which adherence remains powerful, is to treat all teachers as if their performance was similar, even though teachers themselves know that this is not the case. The effects have been to limit incentives for teachers to improve their performance and to make teaching much less attractive to talented and ambitious people than it should be.

70 We are determined to create the conditions for this culture to change. We want to recognise and reward good performance and establish routes for real career progression. We want to reward teachers who are effective and whose pupils make good progress because of the motivation and inspiration they provide. We want to reward teachers who take on tough classes and deal with difficult children, and those who take the able to new heights. We recognise that many people working in schools make a substantial time commitment to carry out their professional duties. We want to reward teachers who contribute, with their expertise and their professional commitment, to raising standards of achievement and to the wider life of the school.

> "Good teachers will ensure that the country has the well educated and skilled young people so necessary for its economic well-being and the future of its society. Accordingly, teachers must be supported by modern leadership, the highest quality training and development programmes, and a professional pay system which reflects their importance."
>
> *David Hart,*
> *General Secretary, National Association*
> *of Head Teachers, November 1998*

71 We therefore propose a pay system with the following objectives:

- it should attract, retain and motivate all staff;

- it should provide greater rewards and faster progress for the best teachers;

- it should enable teachers to progress by excellent classroom performance as well as by taking on management responsibilities;

- decisions on pay should be informed by rigorous annual appraisal;

- there should be greater discretion on decision-making in this area at school level within the national framework;

- school salary policies should be transparent and fair; and

- no serving teacher should lose out on existing entitlements in salary as a result of the change to the new system but higher pay in future should be justified by performance and achievement.

72 The result of implementing a pay system with these objectives will be a significant increase in the salary of many teachers. As we have repeatedly made clear, additional investment over and above the STRB's normal salary reviews must bring modernisation and improved performance in return.

> "Here is one set of realities: the quest for improvement is on. Teachers cannot expect something for nothing. Poor performance cannot be subsidised. In future pay will be linked to performance at the individual class teacher level. A blanket refusal to look at Performance Related Pay is no longer on."
>
> *Bruce Douglas,*
> *former President of*
> *Secondary Heads Association, October 1998*

School level flexibility within a national framework

73 We set out in the paragraphs below how a new system might work. In developing these proposals, we have drawn on valuable work undertaken or commissioned by teacher unions and by the National Employers' Organisation for School Teachers. We have also looked at research on pay in the education systems of other countries and examined developments in other public services and the business sector. We will set out further details of our proposals in the more detailed consultative document on performance management referred to in paragraph 44, to be published early in 1999. This will also look at the complex issues relating to the transition to the new pay system which we would expect to take effect from September 2000.

> "An effective package will demand changes in structure, priorities, expectations and roles, in other words, everything that is needed to complement the professional expertise of our teachers. In return, teachers must expect that extra resources must be matched by high standards and a willingness to challenge existing practices. The public will demand that additional resources are matched by a profession which rewards and retains only those who can meet those demands."
>
> *"A New Deal for Schools", National Employers' Organisation for School Teachers, July 1998*

School level flexibility within a national framework

74 It is our intention that the School Teachers' Review Body (STRB) should continue to make recommendations to government on pay and conditions for teachers nationally. The process it has adopted has worked effectively. Within the national framework, we aim to extend the flexibility which schools need to make the system work in their own circumstances. This is consistent with the overall thrust of our policy to give schools greater freedom and responsibility to improve themselves.

75 We propose a much closer link between pay and appraisal than has previously been the case. A key element of the new arrangements would be the new performance threshold which we envisage would be set at the nine-point maximum currently available for experience and qualifications. It would offer a significant rise in salary after some five to seven years for high performing teachers with a track record of consistently strong performance who are prepared to meet higher professional expectations.

76 Individual teachers' pay might vary according to a number of elements:

- increments awarded subject to satisfactory performance up to a performance threshold;

- a substantial increase in salary for those teachers who cross the performance threshold;

- opportunities for further pay progression for teachers above the threshold determined at school level in the light of their performance and responsibility;

- non-consolidated bonuses, available to all staff, paid in accordance with school pay policy and funded from a new School Performance Award Scheme; and

- salary supplements determined at school level for specific purposes such as recruitment and retention.

77 The sections that follow deal first with our proposals for teacher appraisal, which will be a key factor in determining an individual teacher's pay, and then with different aspects of pay. They apply equally to full-time and part-time teachers.

> "Appraisal or assessment should certainly form a large part of the promotion process. In the 1980s the NASUWT accepted the need for a sensible and fair appraisal system, properly administered, to be constructed in order to identify and reward good practice without the teacher having to leave the classroom."
>
> *Nigel de Gruchy, General Secretary, NASUWT, October 1998*

Teacher appraisal

78 The present statutory scheme of teacher appraisal has become largely discredited because in most schools it has been seen as a pointless additional burden rather than an integral part of the school's performance management arrangements. The Government has already made clear that it wants to introduce a new, properly focused system of teacher appraisal which has clear objectives and outcomes.

> "It is becoming clear that appraisal is most effective where it is integrated with a school's management processes. It means that teachers' agreed objectives can link sensibly with schools' targets; it allows professional development to be properly targeted, planned and resourced; it means that lines of responsibility are clear; it minimises bureaucracy by allowing the maximum use of data and outcomes already available from other sources."
>
> *Estelle Morris,*
> *Minister for School Standards, July 1998*

79 At the heart of all good performance management must be a thorough annual assessment of the performance of every member of staff which should result in the setting of targets for improvement and development over the next year. In the case of teachers, appraisal must include assessment of classroom performance through observation and analysis of the progress their pupils have made.

80 We propose that in future appraisal should:

- take place annually;
- involve classroom observation and other objective evidence of performance;
- take pupil progress into account; and
- result in the setting of individual targets for each teacher, at least one of which should be directly linked to the school's pupil performance targets.

81 We believe that this rigorous new approach should inform decisions about teachers' pay as well as their professional development. It should also strengthen performance reviews for deputies, ASTs and other school leaders. Indeed, the artificial separation of pay and appraisal under the scheme introduced in 1991 explains in large part why it has been seen as marginal and therefore why it has not been taken seriously by either heads or teachers. We recognise that it would be wrong to make crude links between teacher performance and pupil outcomes. Issues such as student mobility, student absenteeism or curriculum changes and variations between subjects need to be taken into account.

82 As our proposals for performance management develop we will want to identify and build on good practice which meets genuine concerns about teacher assessment without losing a clear link with pupil performance. Systems of performance-related pay can become bogged down in bureaucracy. We recognise the risks and will want to ensure that this does not happen. Our intention is that the system itself should be as straightforward and transparent as possible.

Teachers' pay up to the performance threshold

83 We envisage a pay range leading up to the performance threshold. Teachers could normally expect increments in their early years of teaching but their rate of progress would depend on their performance as monitored through induction and annual appraisal. In those rare cases where performance was entirely unsatisfactory the teacher should leave the profession. Teachers who fell below expectations might not gain an increment in one or more years. Excellent performers such as those on the fast-track scheme explained in paragraphs 116-119 might move rapidly up to the threshold with double increments in one or more years.

The performance threshold

84 Some teachers might choose to stay at the threshold pay level. But once they reached the performance threshold, teachers would have the right to apply, if they wished, for a performance assessment. Success would depend on high and sustained levels of competence, achievement and commitment. Successful candidates would need to demonstrate that they had consistently achieved new national standards centred on strong classroom performance. Teachers might be required to apply for assessment more than once if there were doubts about their track record or their preparedness for the level of responsibility involved. Over time, we would expect the majority of our teachers to be of a standard which would allow them to cross the threshold if they wished.

85 The performance threshold would offer the opportunity to advance to a significantly higher professional level, with an immediate salary increase of up to 10 per cent and access to a higher pay range. We will want to seek views about how large the immediate increase should be relative to the upper pay range. Successful teachers would be expected to make a much fuller professional contribution to teaching and learning in the school, including giving more time and commitment to their own professional growth and development and extending learning opportunities for pupils in addition to, as a matter of course, continuing to teach to a high standard.

86 The assessment procedure at the threshold would need to be rigorous and clear. We will consult on the best approach but anticipate that it should involve a combination of external and internal assessment comprising:

- demonstration by the teacher of proven and sustained high quality teaching, resulting in positive outcomes for pupils' performance;
- clear evidence of a commitment to professional development and the impact this has had on classroom performance;

- a robust and careful assessment by the head of the quality of the teacher's performance against the national standards, based on classroom observation and the reports of line managers; and

- a check on the head's judgement by an external assessor, who would review the evidence for every applicant including appraisal judgements, discuss every applicant with the head and observe a sample of candidates.

87 Performance information should be available through the new system of annual appraisal. We would expect headteachers to discuss with the external assessors the evidence about those teachers who were borderline. The assessors would provide the necessary degree of national consistency and monitor the head's overall operation of the new pay system as a whole as well as confirming or challenging decisions on the performance threshold. As suggested in paragraph 45, it would seem sensible for the same external assessor to offer advice to the governing body on the appraisal and pay review of the headteacher. We would want to streamline procedures further by combining performance threshold assessments with those for the Advanced Skills Teacher grade.

> "PAT's submission to the 1997 Pay Review Body sought to balance 'high competence from well qualified professionals on the one hand and proper status and financial reward on the other'... We recognise the need for highly competent teachers, backed up by appropriate support, and also society's right to expect world-class performance from the education system."
>
> *Kay Driver,*
> *General Secretary, Professional Association*
> *of Teachers, July 1998*

Further pay above the threshold

88 We envisage that each teacher above the threshold would be allocated by the governing body to an individual pay range within the upper scale, assigned on a combination of excellent performance and extra responsibility. Heads of departments or subject coordinators have responsibility for the effectiveness of teaching and learning in a given subject or area of activity. Their contribution is crucial and they can only do their job well if they themselves are good teachers.

89 We want to seek views in particular about the way the new arrangements will work above the threshold. We envisage that teachers above the threshold would benefit from any general pay increase awarded on the advice of the School Teachers' Review Body. In addition, the individual pay ranges would give scope to reward sustained high performance in post on the basis of performance review informed by annual appraisal. To retain their eligibility to progress up the range teachers would need to continue to demonstrate good performance and results. A higher pay range could be achieved by moving to a more challenging post or to the leadership tier. Conversely, a teacher would expect to move to a lower pay range in transferring to a less demanding post.

> "We need a can-do culture and a restoration of teachers' corporate professional self-confidence, by which I do not mean complacency. I think this is a huge problem and I do not think it falls to any one person or organisation to solve it. It's something that everybody has got to work very hard at, including the unions."
>
> *Peter Smith,*
> *General Secretary, Association of Teachers*
> *and Lecturers, 1997*

90 There would be higher professional expectations of all teachers above the threshold, as described in paragraph 85, whether or not they took on specific additional responsibilities. We will consult on whether this requires a different, more demanding contract for this group of teachers.

> "The National Union of Teachers welcomes the decision of the Government to address fundamental issues concerning the recruitment, retention and motivation of teachers. The success of the Green Paper will be judged on the extent to which the education of our children is enhanced and teaching becomes the first choice of qualifying graduates."
>
> *Doug McAvoy,*
> *General Secretary, NUT,*
> *November 1998*

Fast-track

91 It is important that the profession makes the most of able and talented recruits. We explain in paragraphs 116-119 our proposals for a new fast-track scheme to identify excellent trainees and teachers and move them rapidly to the threshold. We would expect teachers on the fast-track to reach the threshold more quickly than the norm.

The School Performance Award Scheme

92 We recognise that as well as rewarding professionalism and excellence among individual teachers there is a strong case for rewarding excellence for teams of staff and schools as a whole. We therefore plan to introduce a School Performance Award Scheme. A targeted national fund would be distributed to schools solely for the purpose of offering non-consolidated performance bonuses to staff. The fund would be distributed to the top percentage of schools according to a range of performance indicators. It would reward a significant number of schools each year. A school which demonstrated consistently excellent performance or which improved significantly – if, for example, it was pulled rapidly out of special measures – might expect to receive an award. By contrast, an underperforming school would not, even if its raw exam and test results were apparently good. We will look particularly at ways of identifying which special schools should benefit.

93 We will consult in our detailed document in January 1999 on factors which would best identify school performance and avoid penalising schools for reasons beyond their control. It would be for the head and governors to decide how to distribute the funds among staff, based on the criteria set out in the school's performance management policy. Schools would be expected to reward those staff who had contributed to their success, as teams or individuals, including teaching assistants and other support staff.

Performance management in schools

94 The pay proposals set out in the paragraphs above depend for their fairness on the success of appraisal as part of performance management. Through the school improvement element of the Standards Fund, substantial funding will be available over the next three years to support the introduction of performance management, including training. We want heads to be able to deploy resources more effectively and give them more ways of motivating good teachers.

95 By the same token we look to heads to tackle management problems squarely. Heads and senior managers should manage the performance of teachers on a day to day basis and should be aware of any emerging problems.

Examples

Case 1
A new entrant to the teaching profession would normally reach spine point 9 (£22,410 at December 1998 salaries) in around seven years, and would therefore be at the threshold at approximately age 29. If he or she passed on the first occasion on which he or she was assessed, this teacher would receive an uplift for passing the threshold. Assuming continued good performance, this teacher would then receive further salary increases in his or her post, and could see further pay progression by taking on additional and more challenging objectives.

Case 2
A head of year currently on spine point 11 (£25,215) when the new arrangements are introduced would be able to apply to be assessed for the threshold immediately. Assuming that he or she were successful at the assessment, the teacher would receive an uplift for passing the threshold, and would be placed on the new upper scale at a point which took into account his or her contribution to teaching and learning in the school. He or she would then be able to progress, subject to continuing good performance in the same post, further up the range. There would be opportunities to progress further by taking on more challenging objectives.

Case 3
A fast-track new entrant showing exceptional performance could accelerate to the threshold at spine point 9 (£22,410) by taking two double steps, and might therefore reach the threshold at 27. This teacher could already have been made a subject head, with a commensurate increase in salary. Having passed the threshold assessment, the teacher would be placed on the upper scale at a point reflecting his or her contribution to teaching and learning in the school – eg as head of department. After some years, say at age 33, this teacher might, if continuing to demonstrate excellent performance, be appointed to the leadership group, and receive a significant salary increase in relation to the additional challenges taken on.

The new capability procedures which schools should have in place by the end of 1998 provide for rapid action – leading to dismissal if appropriate – where teachers fall below acceptable standards of competence. The Government is also concerned about rates of absenteeism across the public sector. In teaching the effects can be particularly disruptive and damaging to children's education. We will set targets to reduce levels of sickness absence in schools – as the Government is doing across the public sector as a whole. We will give guidance to school managers through the Healthy Schools Initiative on managing occupational health issues.

Funding

96 The extra resources for education agreed as a result of the Government's spending review took account of pay pressures, including extra resources for teachers' pay which would be fed through to schools as the new system comes into place. We will ensure that at least part of the extra resources are clearly identified in the early years so that governing bodies are confident they have the resources to fund the new system. At the same time we will want to ensure that decisions on pay increases are properly based and provide good value for money. We will consult further in the technical paper on how this is achieved.

Accountability

97 For the new pay and performance management system to operate effectively, it is important that roles and responsibilities of governing bodies and heads are clearly laid down and that the process is open, transparent and accountable. Given the importance of the system, we propose to make it a statutory requirement for governing bodies to have in place an up-to-date performance management policy. We will provide exemplar policies for heads and governing bodies to help them design their own. We will also encourage Local Education Authorities to provide comparative data about school performance, budgets and salaries to inform pay decisions in individual schools.

Teaching awards

To focus press and public attention on the very best practice in schools across England, Lord Puttnam has established, with the support of Lloyds TSB, a charitable Trust to run the 1999 Teaching Awards. The Trustees include representatives of the six teacher unions, and are supported by the three main political parties.

Lord Puttnam said: "The Awards will identify 600 examples of best practice across England, and the BBC will celebrate these teachers at work in their school communities. A teacher is not an island – every teacher is part of a learning community. The Teaching Awards Trust in association with the BBC believes that by recognising individual teachers, a celebration of the whole school will follow. This shows what is possible when private business, teachers, politicians and Government work together.

Awards won't change the world for teachers, but they will go some small way towards recognising how teachers can change the world for others."

98 It is important that schools are held to account for the performance management policy once it has been put in place. The OFSTED inspection framework will need to be revised to take account of the changes in performance management which flow from this Green Paper and of the high priority which the Government attaches to it. We will expect OFSTED inspectors to comment on how the school's performance management system is impacting on standards.

99 We will also ask the Audit Commission to check – on a sample basis – that schools have performance management policies in place to reward staff efficiently and effectively and that they operate pay arrangements with propriety.

Pensions

100 Pensions are an integral part of an employee's remuneration package. We recognise the importance of providing teachers with a pension scheme which provides an appropriate range and level of benefits. We also recognise that some teachers may want to adopt different patterns of working as they approach retirement and that pensions provision should enable us to harness the talent of experienced teachers.

101 We have already made some significant changes to the provisions of the Teachers' Pension Scheme to allow teachers who are approaching the end of their careers to 'step down' to posts of lesser responsibility without any reduction in their pension benefits. Employers can continue to offer early retirement to teachers where they judge it to be the best way to improve standards. We have also introduced greater flexibility for retired teachers who wish to return to teaching while drawing their pension and will consider what more might be done to assist teachers in the years leading up to retirement. Teachers who retire on ill health grounds are able to return to teaching provided that their health has recovered and they are no longer receiving ill health retirement benefits.

102 We are currently reviewing the Teachers' Pension Scheme in conjunction with representatives of teacher and employer organisations. The review is considering how to make the scheme more responsive to the needs of the education service and valued by individual teachers and their employers.

103 We see a real need for pensions provision for teachers to be kept up-to-date; and in particular for any pension related issues arising from consultation on this Green Paper to be considered as part of our review of the Teachers' Pension Scheme.

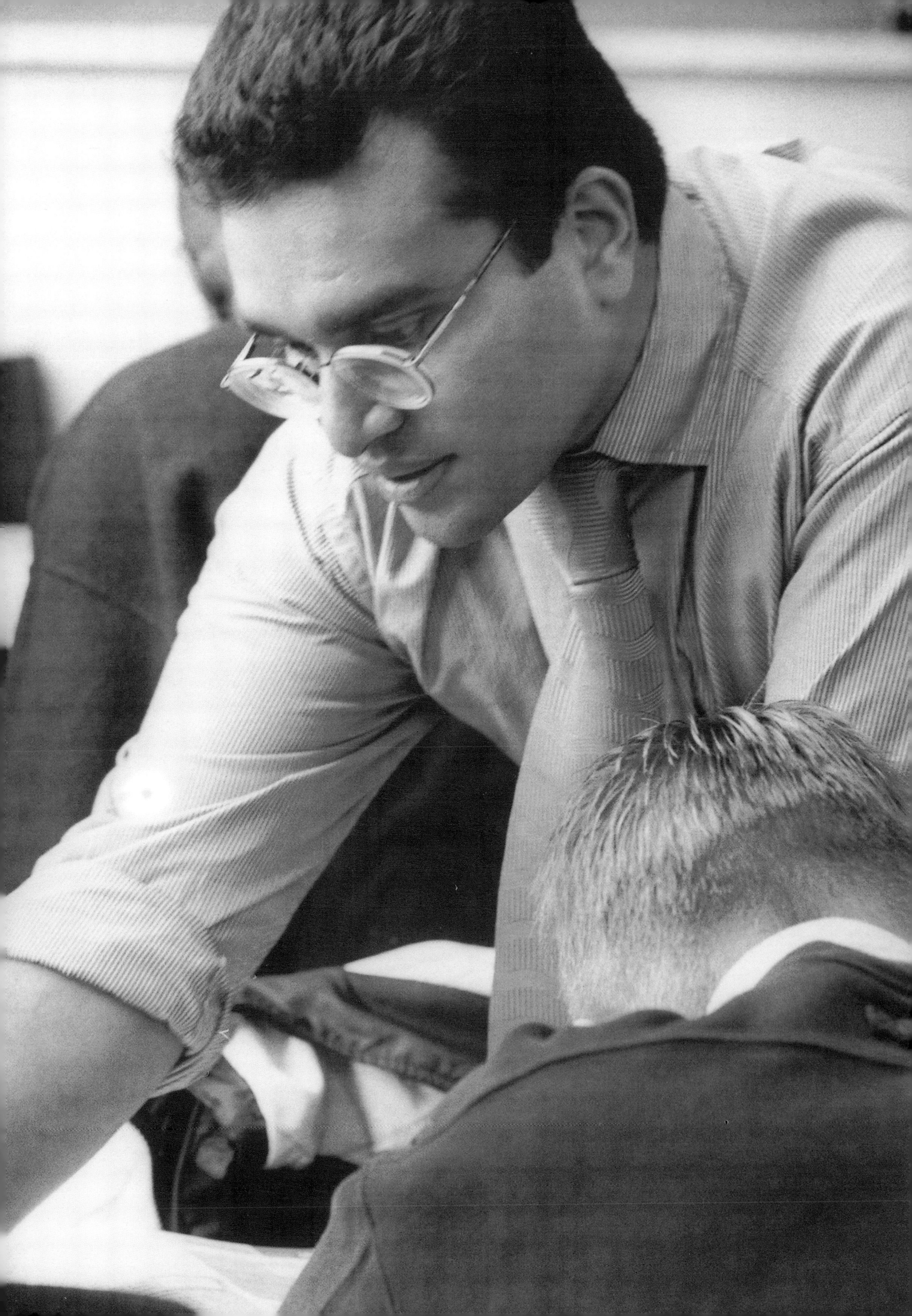

Better training

The Government has set a demanding agenda for high standards. We are committed to giving teachers the training and support they need to do their jobs well and to progress in their careers. We propose further changes are needed to make initial teacher training more flexible and more rigorous and to ensure that all newly qualified teachers have the skills they need. We believe that every teacher has a duty to keep their skills and subject knowledge up-to-date and a right to high quality professional development throughout their careers. Training for classroom assistants should be strengthened.

Key proposals are:

For future teachers

- new national tests for all trainee teachers to guarantee high-level skills in numeracy, literacy and ICT;
- new pre-course provision for trainee teachers;
- review of the procedures for Qualified Teacher Status;
- a network of schools to pioneer innovative practice in school-led teacher training;
- more flexible courses for initial teacher training;
- a boost to employment-based routes into teaching; and
- a new national fast-track scheme to recruit from the best graduates and move outstanding teachers quickly through the profession.

For existing teachers

- a contractual duty for all teachers to keep their skills up-to-date;
- a new focus on professional development bringing together national, school and individual priorities;
- a national Code of Practice for training providers and a new inspection programme to ensure that training gives value for money and delivers results;
- more training out of school hours to minimise disruption to children's education;
- a review of training for supply teachers;
- continued emphasis on equipping teachers with good ICT skills; and
- a new programme of scholarships and international development opportunities.

For other staff

- a pilot of Individual Learning Accounts for all school staff, including teachers;
- use of National Vocational Qualifications to improve the training of teaching assistants; and
- easier ways for teaching assistants to move on to teacher training programmes.

A career of learning

104 We propose that professional standards should provide a framework for individual teachers to plan their professional development throughout their careers. The key milestones will be:

- the standards required for successful completion of training (Qualified Teacher Status);
- the standards required by newly qualified teachers for entry to the profession (Induction);
- the new standards for the proposed performance threshold assessment (paragraph 86);
- the standards for Advanced Skills Teachers; and
- the standards for headship.

Taken together these standards will let teachers see from the start of their career how each step in their training and development fits together.

Initial teacher training

105 We intend to build on the important reforms we have introduced to make initial teacher training more comprehensive and rigorous. A number of institutions are already offering high quality training which provides new teachers with the best possible start. But the standards of training vary widely among institutions. We believe that further change is needed to ensure that all new teachers start their careers having mastered the knowledge and skills they need.

Better quality

106 We have already set in place new national standards which all trainees must have met from May 1998 in order to qualify as teachers. A new national curriculum for initial teacher training specifies the content which all trainees must learn in the core subjects of English, mathematics, science, and in the use of Information and Communication Technology in all subject teaching. All courses must implement these changes in full by September 1999.

107 Every new teacher must have a thorough grounding in literacy, numeracy and ICT skills. The present system does not guarantee this. We propose to introduce skills tests which trainees would have to pass before they could be awarded Qualified Teacher Status (QTS). The tests will be set and examined nationally and could be taken before, during or after training. Given the current concerns about levels of numeracy in schools we propose to pilot a numeracy test from the summer of 1999, for introduction as a national requirement for all those qualifying from summer 2000. Tests in literacy and ICT will be piloted from summer 2000 for national introduction from summer 2001.

108 Some training providers offer extra opportunities for trainees to improve their subject knowledge before the course starts. This sort of pre-course study will become more important in view of the new skills tests. Students should get every help to meet the standards schools need. We will review existing practice on pre-course and in-course study and encourage the development of new provision which might then be offered nationally.

109 OFSTED inspects initial teacher training providers. The Teacher Training Agency has the power to withdraw a provider's accreditation if inspection shows that their training and assessment arrangements do not meet national requirements. This has been a powerful lever in driving up quality but does not ensure that each individual trainee merits the award of Qualified Teacher Status. We want QTS standards to be sharp and consistent across the country, both at the higher education institutions and at their partner schools. We will consult on ways of strengthening the assessment of individual trainees for Qualified Teacher Status. One option would be for the Teacher Training Agency to accredit all external examiners of initial teacher training courses.

Recognising the contribution of schools

110 Most schools contribute to initial teacher training, whether as partner schools with higher education institutions, providers of school-centred training or through training entrants on employment-based routes. This is a valuable investment in the new generation of teachers. We intend to review funding arrangements to ensure that they recognise the role of schools as equal partners. In particular, we will consult on the case for funding the higher education/school partnership directly rather than channelling funding for partner schools through higher education institutions.

111 We want to encourage good and innovative practice in school-led initial teacher training. We will establish a network of high quality training schools, with additional investment in Information and Communication Technology to allow them to give direct on-line advice to trainees, to provide mentor training and to disseminate best practice to satellite schools and to higher education institutions. These schools could also develop a research capability, developing good practice on induction and in-service training.

Extending flexibility

112 Training routes should be diverse and flexible so that training can be matched to the needs and circumstances of all those with the potential to succeed as teachers. Teaching must attract high quality candidates from every section of society, bringing strengths and qualities which ensure that teaching is a vibrant and diverse profession. The Teacher Training Agency is asking all training providers to set targets for the numbers of ethnic minority and male trainees to whom they offer places. We are already seeing a move away from undergraduate study of education (through the Bachelor of Education degree course) to more postgraduate training. Alongside the existing one-year certificate we propose to develop new modular courses for postgraduate teacher training available from 2000, structured in shorter segments and with flexible start and end points. These should be attractive to a wide range of applicants – particularly more mature career changers and re-entrants – who may want to train over a longer period and/or while remaining in their existing job.

113 When the new modules are available, we will ask higher education institutions to look at ways of integrating teacher training modules into their undergraduate degrees so that students could gain experience and recognition by working as paid associates in a school while taking the relevant modules of the teaching course. A maths student, for example, could opt to take some teacher training modules during his or her first degree course and so gain accreditation towards the postgraduate teaching qualification. Such approaches will increasingly break down the barriers between undergraduate and postgraduate training. Some institutions may also want to consider whether existing undergraduate provision might be reshaped to help Qualified Teaching Assistants move on to train to become qualified teachers.

114 We will encourage both graduates and undergraduates to act as part-time teaching associates for which they could be paid as teaching assistants. This would give teachers more adult support and at the same time access to the latest developments in particular subject areas or to particular expertise like the creative arts. It should provide valuable experience for schools and students alike and also enable students to find out first hand whether teaching is a career for them. We intend, from next year, to pilot the use of students as teaching assistants in Education Action Zones.

115 We are determined that employment-based routes into teaching should be recognised as providing high quality preparation for entry into the profession, open to those who may not be able to pursue a more traditional teacher training course. In October 1998 we announced new incentives to schools to accept trainees on these routes and we will encourage the further expansion of such provision. In particular, we want to pilot the possibility of funding students directly, rather than the course providers, so that individual students can put together the elements of training in the way that best suits them.

A national fast-track scheme

116 Teaching should be a career which attracts a greater share of the most talented and offers rapid advancement to teachers of exceptional ability. We propose, therefore, to create a new fast-track scheme which will offer extra training and support to the most promising and enable them to reach the performance threshold more rapidly. In return, fast-track entrants would be asked to accept supplementary contracts which entailed a longer working year and greater mobility. The fast-track would be open both to recruits to initial teacher training and to excellent serving teachers below the threshold.

117 The purpose of the scheme is to attract top quality teachers. This does not mean just academic high-flyers. The scheme will seek to identify those who combine academic ability and high level subject knowledge with the gifts of communication and the ability to inspire. We envisage two possible ways of entering the scheme:

- through a national graduate recruitment scheme; and

- through application by, or nomination of, teachers showing exceptional talent in training or in the early years of teaching.

Employment-based teacher training

The Government's Graduate Teacher Programme enabled Kevin O'Flaherty to switch to teaching after over 20 years in the retail and engineering sectors.

Kevin's interest in teaching began when he did voluntary and, later, paid work as a special needs assistant in a local school. That inspired him to take a degree in educational studies at the University of Hertfordshire, and now his training programme will build on that to develop his knowledge and skills to the standards required for Qualified Teacher Status.

Kevin says: "I decided to move into teaching because it was my belief that children not only benefit from academic tuition but also from life experiences. Being a mature candidate I had considerable work experience; this was augmented with knowledge of children gained by having two teenage daughters. Therefore I felt I was a suitable candidate for the teaching profession."

Our Lady's School, Welwyn Garden City, were delighted when he applied for a trainee post. Headteacher Mrs Brid Regan says, "We have a recruitment problem in the area and we have, with many other schools, a gender issue – many of the children do not have a male role model either at home or at school and we feel that our children would benefit from this appointment."

The Graduate Teacher Programme allows schools to appoint mature people to teaching posts and to train them on the job – to exactly the same standards as other trainee teachers. The Teacher Training Agency manages the programme, working closely with schools, Local Education Authorities and teacher training providers.

118 The recruitment process would be rigorous and searching and based on stringent criteria. We will publicise the scheme widely among graduates and newly appointed teachers. In the longer term up to 5 per cent of teachers might be on the fast-track.

119 We anticipate that entry to the scheme should involve supplementary contractual requirements. They might be expected to commit to a further 4 to 6 weeks contracted time a year. They could be expected to be more mobile than most teachers, to allow them to be deployed in particular schools – those in difficulties for example – which were in urgent need of excellent staff. We will consult on arrangements for the new scheme early in 1999, with a view to piloting some aspects from September 1999.

Support for new teachers

120 Professional development starts when a new teacher first enters school. A statutory induction year will be introduced for those coming new to teaching from September 1999. The starting point for the induction will be the Career Entry Profile which identifies the strengths of each newly trained teacher and his or her priorities for further professional development. The Government will provide the necessary funding to guarantee all new teachers a reduced teaching load and a programme of support to ensure that they have the time to consolidate and improve their performance.

Career and professional development

121 A clear and continuing commitment to professional development throughout a career should be at the heart of teachers' professionalism. The Government is making a very substantial investment in teachers' professional development over the next three years through the Standards Fund to support national training priorities such as literacy, numeracy and school improvement. In addition, the New Opportunities Fund will provide £230million across the UK to ensure that teachers become confident in the use of ICT in subject teaching. The nation – as well as schools and teachers – needs to see a real return on that investment.

122 Much existing training is unsystematic and unfocused. We intend to set out a clear framework for professional development which brings together national, school and individual training priorities to help all teachers to raise standards in the classroom and to progress within the new career structure.

A new training framework

123 To formalise the importance of career and professional development we propose that teachers' contracts of employment should include a duty to keep their skills up-to-date. We would expect this to be reflected in the personal and career development targets for teachers which are agreed as part of the annual appraisal process. There are three distinct, and equally important, elements to be taken into account:

- **national** training priorities focused on particular needs which have been identified nationally e.g. literacy, numeracy, ICT, headship training, special educational needs;

- **school** priorities emerging from school development planning to help schools reach their own targets and implement their post-OFSTED action plans; and

- **individual** development needs of teachers identified through annual appraisal.

We will review existing funding mechanisms to ensure the right balance between sustained focus on national priorities and flexibility to match school and individual needs.

124 As the new professional body for teachers, the General Teaching Council (GTC) will clearly have a key interest in teaching standards and in professional development. Once the GTC is fully established, we would expect it to consider how the proposals in this paper might be reflected in the Code of Practice it will issue to lay down standards of professional conduct and practice expected of registered teachers. The Council may wish to consider whether there should be a professional duty for teachers to keep their skills up to date, which would underpin the new contractual duty. It may also want to consider how teachers' achievements against the new career framework might be recorded on the new national register of teachers.

Monitoring quality

125 We believe that new quality assurance arrangements are needed so that schools and teachers can be confident that training time and money are invested in good quality provision. We will consult on a new national Code of Practice for all major providers of publicly-funded training. It would, for example, require providers to reflect up-to-date research and inspection evidence, to link provision directly to the proposed new career structure, and to include mechanisms for monitoring and evaluating the impact on pupil performance.

126 The Teaching and Higher Education Act gives OFSTED a new statutory right to inspect and report on the quality of any in-service training provided for school teachers from public funds. We intend to ask OFSTED, in consultation with the Teacher Training Agency, to draw up proposals for a rolling programme of inspection of existing provision by Local Education Authorities, training institutions and private training providers. Teachers' views on the provision available should play a significant part in that inspection process.

The General Teaching Council (GTC)

The General Teaching Council will be the new statutory professional body for teachers. It will be a key partner in the Government's drive to raise standards.

Teachers will make up a majority of the Council's members, which will also include people appointed by major representative bodies in education and by the Secretary of State.

The GTC will:

- prepare a Code of Practice laying down standards of professional conduct and practice expected of registered teachers;

- maintain a register of qualified teachers, and teachers in maintained schools will be required to register, paying a modest annual fee;

- have powers to strike a teacher off its register on the grounds of unacceptable professional conduct or serious professional incompetence; and advise the Secretary of State on misconduct cases which arise from child protection concerns;

- hear any appeals against decisions by Local Education Authorities that a newly qualified teacher had failed to pass their induction year; and

- advise the Secretary of State and others on a wide range of teaching issues: from recruitment and supply; through training and induction; to professional development and conduct. The GTC will have a major role to play in advising on teacher training and the Secretary of State will be required to consult the GTC on any future change in standards required for entry to the profession.

The GTC will be an authoritative professional voice. It will give teachers the opportunity to regulate their own profession and influence the way it develops. The Council will be established by the year 2000.

127 Too often those schools facing the greatest challenges in teaching their pupils are also faced with the highest turnover of staff and the greatest problems in filling vacancies. They therefore rely significantly on the role which supply teachers are able to play in supporting pupils' learning and maintaining school standards. It is therefore essential – and long overdue – that the training given to supply teachers is of the same high standard as for other serving teachers. We intend to review the existing arrangements for the training, performance management and employment of supply teachers to ensure that they have the skills and knowledge we expect of all teachers in the modernised profession. We will discuss these important issues with Local Education Authorities and the private companies that employ supply teachers. We will take action where we believe it is needed.

Professional commitment

128 We are concerned that a high proportion of training currently takes place within school time, disrupting children's education and undermining school performance. That must change. The use of supply teachers to cover training should be kept to a minimum. We do not propose to extend formally the classroom teachers' contract beyond the five non-teaching days already provided for each year – but we want to see these used effectively to minimise the need for training in the school year. Where teachers are expected to take training courses outside directed time it is right that they should be paid for doing so. National pay arrangements already allow for this. However, teachers should also see it as part of their professional responsibilities to keep their skills up to date and develop their own effectiveness by being ready to undertake a significant amount of training outside school time – as many already do.

129 Many teachers also make a significant investment in their own personal development, for example by taking MA or doctoral degrees. Within the new career structure, we would expect to see all teachers taking a greater responsibility for contributing to this sort of training cost, particularly once they are above the performance threshold. We would want to offer additional support to those on lower earnings and at the start of their careers. We intend to pilot in the year 2000 new opportunities for using Individual Learning Accounts to encourage the professional development of teachers, classroom assistants and support staff. Ultimately we hope all staff in schools will have Individual Learning Accounts.

Individual Learning Accounts

Denise Lievers, formerly a self-employed childminder, opened her SkillAccount[1] to save towards the cost of NVQ Childcare and Education level 3. She enrolled on the course in March 1996 and completed and gained the certificate in March 1997. The contribution made by Gloucestershire TEC enabled her to pay the full course fees. Having 'caught the learning bug', Denise continued to save regularly and enrolled to take an Assistant Swim Teachers Certificate, part of which was paid for with a £50 'TEC SkillAccount Bonus'.

She has since found employment with a primary school in the Stroud area where she recently started work. Denise says that her SkillAccount gave her the confidence to continue training, helped her to plan for her future (she is still saving) and contributed to her employment as a Teaching Assistant.

[1] SkillAccounts are only available from The Link Group (formerly Gloucestershire Training and Enterprise Council). They form one of thirteen development projects currently operating in England and Wales. Lessons learned from these projects will help inform a national system of accounts. Individual Learning Accounts will start to become available nationally from Spring 1999.

Training for the fast-track

130 Teachers on the new fast-track scheme would be required to undergo a more intensive programme of personal development than other new teachers, beginning with a 'booster' programme during the summer before they start their fast-track post. This would focus on teaching excellence and leadership skills and include some experience of business such as, for example, a two week management placement in the private sector. Fast-track teachers would be expected to do similar work placements or training in following years and might be supported to work towards further professional and/or academic qualifications.

131 Teachers on the fast-track would be expected to change jobs relatively frequently in the early years of their career, to ensure they gained wide and varied experience. If their performance merited it they would be expected to reach the performance threshold more rapidly than most, perhaps in five years: The scheme will be flexible enough to let teachers take time out for domestic reasons and to ensure that mobility is compatible with individual family circumstances.

ICT training

132 Training can be particularly cost-effective and accessible if delivered directly by ICT to the school. The Government is making a major investment in training and equipment, as well as setting up the infrastructure of the National Grid for Learning and developing the Virtual Teachers' Centre. We are now building up a library of resources and practical tools. We are placing advice on best practice, schemes of work and lesson plans on the Standards Site for teachers to access and customise. We will be encouraging the development of ICT-based networks to let teachers share teaching materials and to exchange professional information.

133 The £230 million funding for teacher training across the UK is intended to let every teacher reach the ICT standard set out in the National Curriculum for initial teacher training. Once this baseline is established, we will want to consider how teachers can build on this foundation and go

---

The Standards Site

This internet site (http://www.standards.dfee.gov.uk) is managed by DfEE's Standards and Effectiveness Unit. It aims to help schools improve their effectiveness and reduce workload.

This site provides:

- practical guidance on raising standards, supported by research and inspection evidence. Areas covered include action planning, target-setting, study support, schools under special measures and teacher appraisal;

- internet access to primary Schemes of Work;

- the National Literacy Strategy's Framework for Teaching and information on the Literacy Hour. More than 500 literacy lessons are available at the press of a button;

- national pupil performance information to help schools assess their performance and to set targets;

- a discussion forum, allowing teachers to share with each other their experiences in implementing strategies for raising standards and to tell a wide audience about their successes; and

- video clips in which schools talk about their efforts to raise standards.

The content of the Standards Site will be built up over time as further useful material becomes available.

beyond the standards of the ICT skills test for new teachers. We want to train teachers not only to use ICT for teaching, but also to understand when to use it and when not to use it.

> Earlier this year the Government made £23million available to supply 9,500 internet-ready laptop computers to 9,500 teachers. The laptops are now with the teachers nominated for the programme. Priority was given to Headteachers and Deputy Headteachers because of their importance to improving standards and the development of ICT within the school. Priority was also given to those teachers supporting the literacy and numeracy strategy and supporting teacher training.

External development

134 As in other professions, we believe that experienced and excellent teachers should have opportunities to undertake development or research work to extend and enhance their performance. We intend to review the existing opportunities for study leave, sabbaticals and teacher researchers as a basis for establishing from 2000 a new national programme of scholarships to be open to teachers at all levels in the new professional structure with the outcomes disseminated widely. We are encouraging greater business involvement in schools through new arrangements for tax relief announced in November 1998. Teacher placements in business have two-way benefits in improving awareness in industry of what is happening in education and giving teachers and young trainees valuable outside experience and better awareness of the needs of industry and commerce.

135 With the approach of the millennium, schools are increasingly part of a wider international community. In a world-class service, we will need many more teachers with direct experience of other education systems. The ICT revolution is opening up communication between schools across the globe and the modern teaching force should have clear opportunities to contribute to and learn from other school systems. We intend to review the existing, limited teacher exchange activities and to establish from 2000 a new programme of international development opportunities for teachers and heads, encompassing study visits, exchanges, and short and long-term placements overseas, linked directly to our national training priorities and to the career development of individual teachers. By 2002 we envisage that up to 5,000 teachers annually might have the opportunity to benefit from some form of international professional development.

> **Education Business Partnership/Teacher Placement**
>
> Diana MacAdie of St Gregory's RC Comprehensive School, Tunbridge Wells said, "I feel privileged to have taken part. The time I spent at the company was rich in experiences and awash with scientific principles. The benefits are enormous and are ongoing"
>
> Diana spent a week at Kent Salads as part of the teacher placement into business programme. She and other teachers on placement at other food suppliers had the objective to gather information and materials for use in teaching science at Key Stages 3 and 4. The outcomes will be compiled into curriculum resource materials sponsored by Marks and Spencer. Back at school, she is using the experience to illustrate her teaching and is to invite the company into the school to talk to her pupils about the company's work. She says that she has been greatly influenced by her placement and that "my teaching of the genetics option for A-level Biology will never be quite the same again!"

Teaching assistants

136 Training for teaching assistants is uneven and sometimes poor. The extent and quality of training varies widely from one Local Education Authority to another and there is an equally wide range of qualifications. We propose to work with Local Education Authorities and the relevant agencies to develop an overall training framework, based on National Vocational Qualifications, which would clarify how the various types of training and qualifications fit together, including across the various specialist areas such as early years care, special educational needs, literacy, numeracy or ICT. We do not wish to constrain the range or variety of teaching assistants but we do want them all to have good quality training opportunities.

137 Nursery nurses play a particularly valuable role in the education of young children, often working in a team with the teacher in a nursery class. Here too a better structured and more widely understood framework of qualifications will lead to an improved career structure and better prospects in the profession. Work is well underway on a new qualifications framework for early years education, childcare and playwork, led by the National Training Organisations and the Qualifications and Curriculum Authority. For teaching assistants as a whole we will want to seek views on whether it is sensible to work towards a modular approach with a core set of competences which would be recommended for most assistants and then specialist modules for those working on specific areas such as literacy or numeracy, or supporting pupils with special educational needs.

138 We want to make it easier for teaching assistants to become qualified teachers. The more flexible employment-based routes proposed in paragraph 115 will help. We will want to ensure that credit is given for the experience teaching assistants will have acquired. The Teacher Training Agency have already been asked to report on the development of ways for classroom assistants to move more easily onto teacher training programmes. We are ready to provide funding to take this further forward.

Case Study

Barking and Dagenham Local Education Authority addressed a history of low mathematics and numeracy attainment in the Borough by researching teaching methods in countries where 10-year-olds often out-perform their English counterparts. In 1995, over 50 teachers visited Switzerland and Germany to observe and record pedagogy. In the resultant pilot project, 850 Barking and Dagenham 9-year-olds were taught using a Swiss approach, key elements of which were:

- whole-class teaching, emphasising speech and discussion by pupils;
- an emphasis on thinking skill and on consolidation of learning;
- detailed guidance for teachers; and
- individual pupils leading lessons.

The project involved translating teachers' manuals and producing detailed notes on lesson content and teaching methods, worksheet and transparencies; and delivering in-service training for participating teachers. It is now used in 35 Barking and Dagenham schools and, by 2001, will run from Year 1 to the end of Key Stage 2. Sixteen schools in Leeds have now joined the initiative.

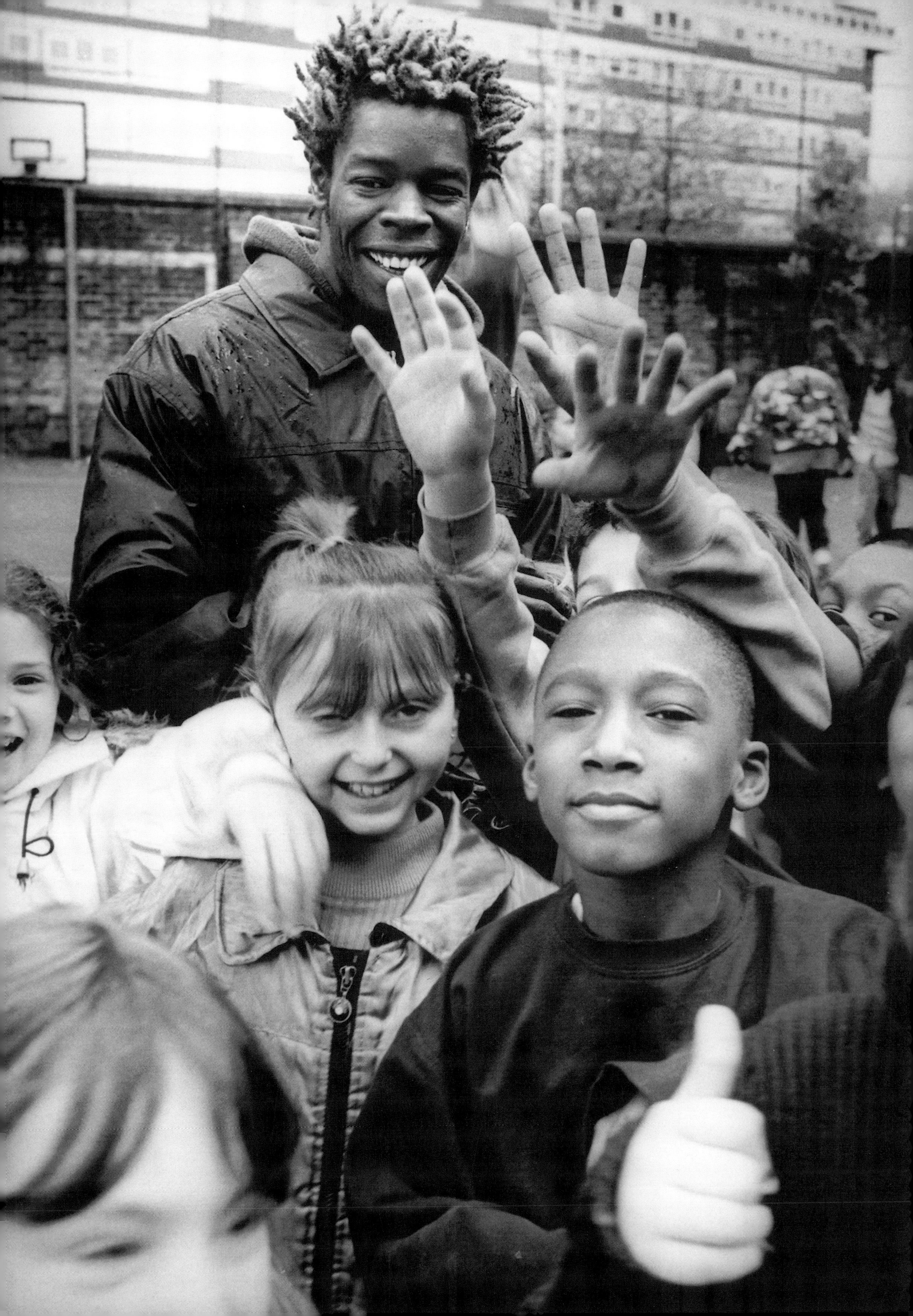

Better support and new possibilities

Teaching and learning can be strengthened by using the full potential of teaching assistants and school support staff. All staff should be fully integrated into the schools' activities – enhancing their own role and giving teachers support and Information and Communication Technology can open up new ways of learning as well as streamlining school administration and helping cut down bureaucratic burdens. Teachers should have working conditions comparable to other professions.

Key proposals are:

- an increase of 20,000 in the number of full-time teaching assistant posts by 2002;
- spreading good and innovative practice in the use of teaching assistants;
- better performance management of classroom assistants and support staff helped by schemes such as Investors in People;
- more efficient administrative and technical support in schools;
- a further drive to reduce bureaucratic burdens on teachers;
- developing the potential of Information and Communication Technology to improve teaching and learning;
- a Small School Support Fund to encourage closer collaboration among small schools; and
- improvements in staff's working environment.

139 The Green Paper will involve important new responsibilities for heads, teachers and for governing bodies. We believe these are essential to make full use of teachers' talents and those who work with them. We will support the introduction of the new performance management system. But we also want to take a series of practical steps to help schools operate more efficiently.

140 Many schools have found effective new ways of operating by rethinking school management, by making better use of other adults in the classroom or by sharing or buying-in services. Teachers tell us that one of the most frustrating aspects of their work is the constant distraction from the core business of teaching. Better support in the classroom will let teachers concentrate their time where it will add most value to pupils' education. Over time we expect schools to become increasingly flexible about the way they use resources, creating effective new combinations of professional teachers, support staff and Information and Communication Technology.

> "Support staff should be seen as integral and valued members of the school team. They are key participants in the drive to raise standards. Without their hard work and dedication, teachers would not be able to concentrate on the vital job of teaching the nation's children."
>
> *Rodney Bickerstaffe*
> *General Secretary, UNISON, November 1998*

Qualified Teaching Assistants

141 Teaching assistants are playing an increasingly important role in schools on tasks such as literacy support and helping pupils with special educational needs. We want that contribution to be fully acknowledged for the first time. We have already allocated £20 million from April 1999 as a pilot to recruit and train the equivalent of 2,000 extra literacy assistants. We will provide an additional 20,000 full-time (or equivalent) assistants for schools by 2002.

142 The numbers of teaching assistants has grown by almost 50 per cent in the last five years. This growth has not, by and large, been matched by opportunities for training and development. There has been little analysis of how teachers can use people working alongside them most effectively. OFSTED evaluation shows

---

Whitmore High School, Harrow

At Whitmore High School for 11-16 year old pupils, the learning support department has 12 learning support assistants who support classes as well as individual students. Forty three pupils have statements of special educational needs and 200 are on the special needs register. Students come to the learning development base for help with homework. Assistants work across the curriculum, across year groups and try to divide their support across the departments. Joint planning is important and once a week support assistants attend a meeting to discuss the use of learning support and to agree expectations and requirements with the teaching staff.

The whole school is committed to defining clear roles for classroom assistants and using their time effectively. The school provides training and a clear career structure. The benefits have been documented by OFSTED, whose recent report on the school commented on the positive impact of the assistants both on curriculum provision and staff morale.

Chapter 5: Better support and new possibilities 57

how significant an impact literacy assistants can have when they have a clearly defined role in the classroom. With the large growth in numbers promised we need to plan for every teaching assistant to have a clear role, good training and real opportunities for career development.

143 We will produce guidance on the use of teaching assistants based on existing good and innovative practice. This should help heads and the teachers who will manage teaching assistants on a day-to-day basis. We will learn from experience with the literacy strategy where we will be training primary teachers in this way from 1999. Assistants will provide an important new resource for teachers to use in their developing role as managers of learning. We would welcome views on the new possibilities opened up by this higher adult:pupil ratio in schools.

144 In most cases pay and conditions for classroom assistants, including nursery nurses, are determined by schools after discussion with Local Education Authorities based on a system of job evaluation. Where schools are the direct employer they negotiate contracts and salaries for individual jobs themselves. In either case it is right that schools should have flexibility to tailor assistants' posts to their own needs. We will discuss with local government representatives and other relevant parties how arrangements for job evaluation accommodate the range of assistants' functions. Assistants' pay should reflect their duties and responsibilities. We will also encourage employers to develop more systematic performance management arrangements.

145 We will encourage both graduates and undergraduates to act as part-time teaching associates for which they could be paid as teaching assistants. This would provide additional adult support to teachers and better access to the latest developments in key school subjects. As suggested in paragraphs 113-114 this could provide course credits towards graduate or postgraduate degrees,

---

Clapton School, East London

Clapton School gained Investors in People recognition in November 1996. The school, which caters for girls from diverse ethnic and religious backgrounds, decided to go for Investors in People to motivate all its staff to increase their professionalism and skills; consolidate and extend their staff development programme; help develop a corporate identity; and raise achievement. There was strong commitment from the headteacher and the Senior Management Team who believe that staff development equates to school development. The benefits included:

- performance reviews for support staff;
- an identified budget share to enhance support staff training;
- awareness of the need to set measurable targets;
- awareness of the need to monitor and evaluate progress;
- a willingness to improve;
- an in-house Management Development Programme; and
- the development of a community of learners, working to a common objective.

In 1997, Clapton School came second in *The Observer's* national school league. Headteacher Cheryl Day said, "The school has undoubtedly improved for staff and pupils alike since we became recognised as an Investor in People. Our in-house Management Development Programme has significantly improved the skills and professionalism of all staff. The children have reaped the benefits."

work experience for the students and give them a taster of teaching as a potential career.

Whole school planning

146 We will continue to encourage schools to become Investors in People which is an important way of helping them address the training and development needs of all staff. Schools are more likely to succeed when every member of staff, regardless of their role, understands what the school is seeking to achieve and what they can do to contribute. Each should have a plan for training and development and be involved in the development of school policies. This has a number of practical implications, including, for example, seeking to enable teaching assistants, including those who are part-time, to be involved in the school's training days and looking imaginatively at ways of developing the role of clerical administrative staff, caretakers, technicians and other support staff so that the whole school community works together to raise standards. The new category of governor for support staff, which we have already put in place, will help to drive this message home.

Volunteers

147 Many people offer support to schools on a temporary or voluntary basis. The most obvious example are the 300,000 school governors who give a great deal of time and energy to carry out their statutory responsibilities and often make a contribution far beyond them. Other volunteers include parents, and sometimes grandparents, prepared to listen to children read, and volunteers from business who act as mentors to heads, staff or pupils, provide work placements or simply provide additional expertise. Good schools value these community resources, manage them well and link them to the school's development plan.

School management and administration

148 Good schools ensure they make full use of the skills of all their staff and think carefully about using outside professionals in areas such as administration, finance, ICT, technical support and pupil welfare. This is usually a far more efficient and cost-effective way of handling non-teaching matters than by adding to the duties of teaching staff. Schools which do not have enough work to make it sensible to have support of their own may want to consider grouping together to share support or to contract it out.

149 Research for the DfEE's Working Group on Reducing the Bureaucratic Burden on Teachers identified a number of administrative tasks often carried out by teachers – collecting money, bulk photocopying, copy typing, standard letters, attendance analysis or copying out lists. The Department is working with teachers, Local Education Authorities and the private sector to find ways of helping schools streamline their administrative systems. A demonstration project with fourteen schools in Derby and Kent will identify good practice and develop a tool-kit which other schools can use to review their own management and administration.

150 The Department is reviewing its own practices to reduce bureaucratic burdens on schools and communicate with them more effectively. Schools have welcomed the new practice of sending DfEE publications in batches with a coversheet summarising contents and action. Exceptions are made only for documents of great importance such as this Green Paper and time critical material such as the performance tables.

151 Further work is in hand to reduce the number of publications sent to schools. A pilot project to send DfEE communications to schools and Local Education Authorities electronically will

> **A Low-Bureaucracy School in 2002**
>
> It is September 2002. At "Lower Burden School":
>
> - all staff are trained in ICT and have ready access to a computer networked into the school management database and the National Grid for Learning;
>
> - a trained administrative assistant ensures that the management information system is kept up-to-date so that data returns can be done at the push of a button, produces statistical reports to help the headteacher and governing body set targets, prepares the basic numerical content of pupil reports, which are then e-mailed to the relevant teachers for personal comment, and generates school timetables using specialist planning software;
>
> - the headteacher has direct access to guidance and statistics on the internet. Model school policies can be downloaded onto the school's Intranet and tailored as necessary; and
>
> - teachers record pupil attendance and performance by inputting the data once only into the school's management information system. When a pupil transfers to another school, their electronic record is made available immediately to the new school via e-mail.
>
> These are extracts from an initial description developed at a seminar of teachers and private sector experts. The description is available for comment on the National Grid for Learning: http://www.dfee.gov.uk/burden/vision.htm, and will be developed further on the basis of good practice from the demonstration project schools in Kent and Derby City.

run from January to March 1999. Initially, two Local Education Authorities and 20 schools will be included in the project although participation will be open to schools and authorities all over the country. The pilot will explore the potential of electronic communication to reduce the quantity of paper DfEE sends schools and authorities in line with central government targets largely to eliminate paper based administrative communication by 2002.

The impact of Information and Communication Technology

152 As chapter one makes clear, the benefits to schools of Information and Communication Technology go well beyond administration. Until recently, the application of ICT has been patchy, with some schools at the cutting edge of technological development and others far behind. The Government wants every school to be able to grasp the new opportunities. By early in the new century new technology will transform every school's administrative systems and its links with the outside world and above all its teaching and learning. All children must be familiar with and competent on the hardware and software and develop the skills they need for their future life.

153 In November 1998 the Prime Minister announced an investment of over £700 million expenditure on Information and Communication Technology for UK schools. This will form an integrated programme with the £230 million already available under the National Lottery's New Opportunities Fund for teacher and librarian training. This investment which is one of the largest committed by any government in the world, will fund an integrated strategy called 'Open for Learning, Open for Business'. The Prime Minister challenged all stakeholders in the use of ICT in schools to respond to that challenge, urging:

- **teachers** to use this investment in technology to raise standards and to take advantage of

Chapter 5: Better support and new possibilities

> **National Grid for Learning**
>
> The Government has adopted the following targets for the National Grid for Learning:
>
> - by 1998 the Government will have started implementing the Grid – target met;
>
> - by 1999 all Newly Qualified Teachers will be ICT-literate to mandatory standards to receive the award of Qualified Teacher Status – target in place;
>
> - by 2002 serving teachers should feel confident and be competent to teach using ICT within the curriculum;
>
> - by 2002 all schools, colleges, universities and libraries and as many community centres as possible should be connected to the Grid, enabling 75 per cent of teachers and 50 per cent of pupils and students to use their own e-mail addresses by then;
>
> - by 2002 most school leavers should have a good understanding of ICT, based firmly on the standards prescribed in the curricula operating in the various parts of the UK, and there should be measures in place for assessing the level of school leavers' competence in ICT;
>
> - by 2002 the UK should be a centre for excellence in the development of networked software content for education and lifelong learning, and a world leader in the export of learning services; and
>
> - from 2002 general administrative communications to schools by the UK Education Departments, OFSTED and non-departmental public bodies, and the collection of data from schools, should largely cease to be paper-based.

the training programme when it starts next year;

- **Local Education Authorities** to develop local plans;

- **business** to innovate and develop products that will support teachers; and

- **pupils and other learners** to use the Grid both as a learning resource and to improve their ICT skills.

New possibilities for teaching and learning

154 Innovative schools are already showing how their work can be transformed by new combinations of teachers and other staff using the potential of Information and Communication Technology. For example:

- schools are using technology and more flexible staffing to vary group sizes, to provide additional support for particular groups of pupils who need it and to enhance the quality of lessons. Research indicates that Information and Communication Technology, used well, can help motivate children;

- a combination of Advanced Skills Teacher, other teachers, support staff and ICT can strengthen teaching in particular subjects; and

- business people or university researchers could agree to be contacted electronically when pupils were undertaking research in a particular area, acting as friends and supporters of a school without ever setting foot in it. E-mail not only removes physical barriers between people, it removes structural barriers and lets pupils work be judged on its merits without reference to their age or status.

St Matthew's RC High School, Manchester

St Matthew's RC High School in Manchester is using ICT links to enable an outstanding technology teacher to provide technology tuition to all its feeder primary schools. The expert is also training the primary staff who support his work. Tuition takes place primarily in the Summer term when the technology teacher's time is freed up by pupils having completed GCSE courses. OFSTED has inspected all the primary schools involved and commented on the success of the scheme. Pupils have made a head start in technology and the primary teachers have gained skill and confidence in teaching technology themselves.

Schools working in partnership

155 Local partnerships and collaboration are an important means of sharing good practice and extending learning opportunities. New communications technology can greatly enhance well established links between secondary schools and their feeder primaries, or between infant and junior schools or paired single-sex schools.

156 The exchange of good practice is at the heart of our proposals for outreach work by Advanced Skills Teachers, specialist teachers for special educational needs, specialist schools and Beacon Schools. Education Action Zones will trial new ways in which schools can work together to tackle problems. The special school in an area could provide expertise to schools integrating pupils with special educational needs and coaching for

The Sir Bernard Lovell School, Bristol

Since the Sir Bernard Lovell School became a Language College in 1996 there has been a strong emphasis on integrating Information and Communication Technology into language teaching programmes. Students make regular use of 75 computers with facilities for independent learning so that whole-class, small group and individual multimedia language work can take place simultaneously.

ICT links with others outside the school form an important part of the work:

- 10 partner primary schools have introduced French into their curriculum, following the success of a pilot project involving multimedia language learning. Primary school teachers now regularly bring their classes to the Sir Bernard Lovell School to work in the main computer suite;

- at post-16 level, the school works closely with a consortium of secondary schools which is soon to pilot the use of video conferencing to deliver aspects of A' level modern foreign language courses; and

- joint bi-lingual projects have been agreed with partner schools in France, Germany and Italy to cover different areas of the curriculum, including science and technology. E-mail and video conferencing will play a major part in this international work.

Sir Bernard Lovell School makes extensive use of Foreign Language Assistants. One has been employed jointly with the partner primary schools to support the pilot primary project. Others work intensively with post-16 students alongside teachers in the classroom and provide tutorials to individual students.

The use of ICT, multimedia learning and Foreign Language Assistants at Sir Bernard Lovell School has contributed to a significant improvement in GCSE languages examination results (1996: 24 per cent A*-C, 1998: 49 per cent A*-C).

> **Applemore College, Hampshire**
>
> Applemore College has been a Technology College since 1994 and has a strong commitment to sharing expertise and resources with neighbouring schools and the local community.
>
> Applemore has been at the forefront of the use of broad band communications in schools, involving pioneering both video conferencing and distance learning techniques, including the use by students of the latest electronic whiteboard technology. Students develop an independent learning style, and are confident in working collaboratively through application sharing, data transferring and manipulation. This extends across all aspects of the curriculum and to all age groups through to the sixth form.
>
> The College's Distance Learning Centre is a good example of partnership with private investment. Students receive and tutors deliver a portfolio of courses at GCSE and advanced level. These are delivered to 60 schools and colleges, involving 130 courses to over 1,000 students.

teachers and learning support assistants. Local Education Authorities have an important function in encouraging collaboration within families of schools.

157 We want to see more schools providing learning opportunities for people of all ages, including the parents of children at the school. Many outward looking schools already play a full part as centres of lifelong learning, opening up specialist facilities to their local community and linking with other education providers such as adult or further education.

Support for small schools

158 Small schools can get particular advantages from sharing teaching expertise to improve standards. As suggested in paragraph 61, some small schools may see advantage in federating under a single head. While we believe every school site needs a teacher who is responsible for teaching and learning at that site, we think there could be considerable educational benefits from such federations.

159 Sharing services can relieve the hard-pressed heads of small schools and enable them to concentrate on raising standards. Services which are not cost-effective for one small school may make sense when they are pooled with other schools – whether financial support, facilities management schemes or the provision of professional development. It could let schools provide more family friendly services such as shared creche facilities.

> **The Dunbury First School, Dorset**
>
> In Dorset co-operative working has been formalised – a 'federated' school (The Dunbury First School) is operating in the Winterbourne Valley. Originally four first schools with falling rolls, each school closed and a single school opened operating on four sites. It has a single governing body and a single headteacher. Accountability is clear.
>
> Staff, parents and pupils have all benefited. Each village has retained its school building and a sense of school identity. Close links with the parish and community are retained and young children continue to enjoy their formative years of education close to home. The federated school has attracted a high quality management team of people keen to pursue this challenge and get the best from those involved. Morale has improved with internal organisational changes such as regular staff meetings and a new more flexible staffing structure. The management structure is more effective and streamlined and takes advantage of economies of scale.

160 Technician support plays an increasing part in the backup services provided to teachers and assistants in the classroom. This is particularly true with the development of new technology, its implementation and maintenance. Larger schools are in a position to take in, full-time or part-time, a dedicated member of staff but others are not. Where small schools are not in a position to take on technical staff full-time or part-time we suggest that urgent steps are taken at local level to consider how schools could jointly fund and share technical help, as with other services such as financial expertise.

161 Some schools may want to go further towards the concept of a 'one-stop' community service bringing together education and other services on a single site with one manager leading the combined operation. As government policies such as the New Deal for Communities begin to make an impact we want the staffing arrangements for schools to be flexible enough to make possible this kind of 'joined-up thinking' at local level. A primary school might be linked with an Early Excellence Centre, adult and community education, health services, and social services, each having their own professional leader responsible to the overall manager. Some experiments in Education Action Zones are already pointing in this direction.

162 Small schools may have least scope in their budgets to invest in these sorts of change. We intend to establish a Small School Support Fund to help pilot innovative approaches. The criteria governing the fund will encourage small schools to invest in shared resources, to work together in some form of federation when this is right to improve educational standards or to combine schools with other services.

The working environment for teachers

163 The Government has promised a major programme of capital investment in schools up to 2002. Annual capital investment in schools will more than double over the life of this Parliament. Each Local Education Authority is being encouraged to produce an Asset Management Plan. In our guidance we want Local Education Authorities to plan systematically to secure and maintain sound buildings which are suitable for teaching and learning. We will ensure that these Plans cover staff as well as pupil accommodation.

> The Government warmly supports a new initiative by Lord Puttnam to research, design and create the 'Staffroom of the Future'. This initiative will take the form of a design competition, run in association with the *Times Educational Supplement*. Lord Puttnam is working with a number of internationally recognised British designers, including Sir Terence Conran and Sir Richard Rogers to work in conjunction with teachers on a brief for the competition.
>
> Up to six entries will be published in the *TES* and teachers will be encouraged to vote for their preferred option, commenting on the nature of a staff workstation. Private sponsorship will be secured to enable the winning design to be constructed in a number of pilot schools, to be chosen from the teacher responses received to the competition.

164 We are determined that teachers and support staff should have better working conditions. In addition, we propose a specific targeted fund for the sole purpose of improving staff working environments and ensuring that teachers have ready access to the equipment they need to work effectively.

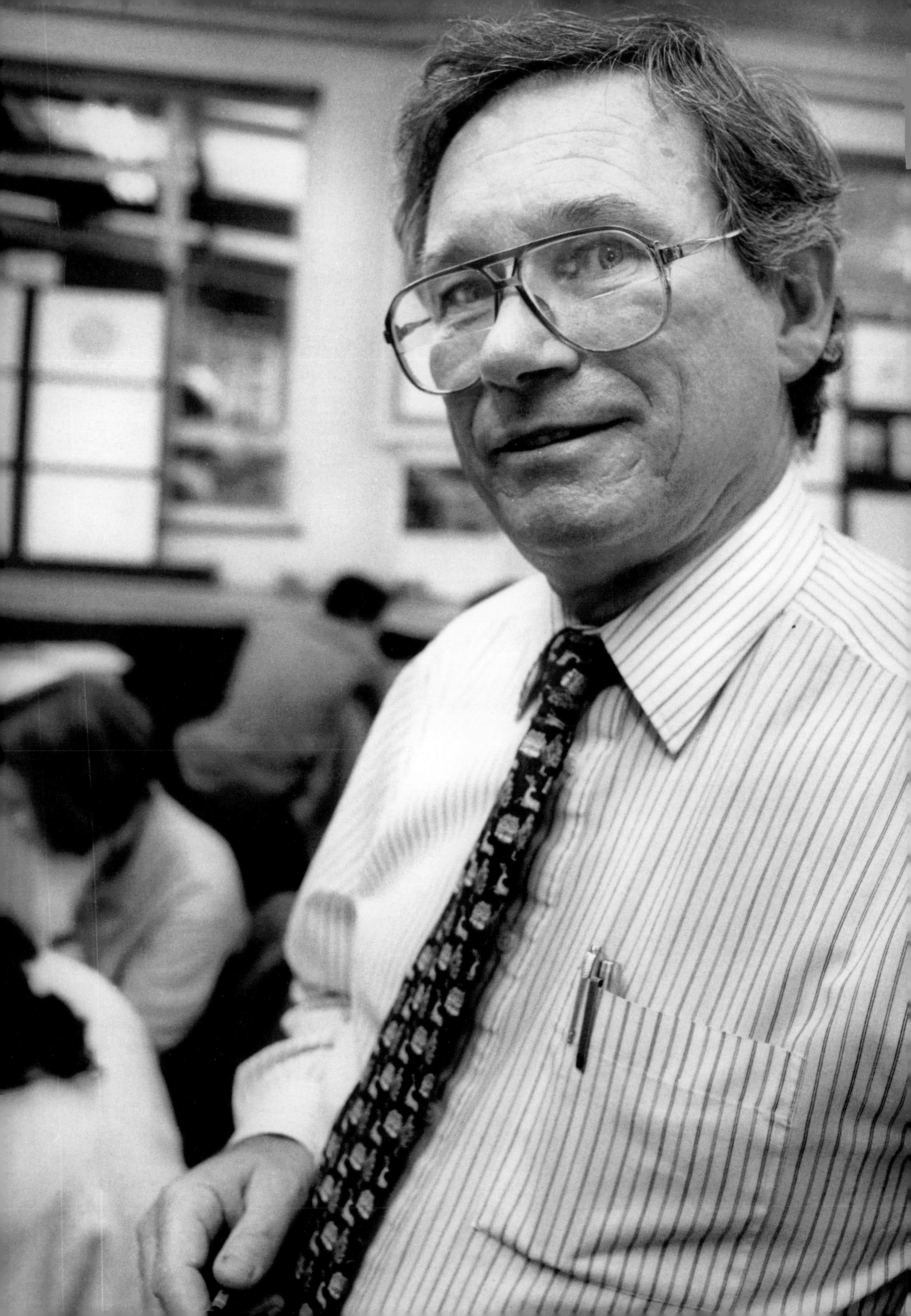

Conclusion

Chapter 6: Conclusion

165 In this Green Paper we have set out an ambitious strategy to strengthen teachers' professionalism, raise standards of achievement for children and help create a world-class education service. This Green Paper is being published only for the teaching profession in England. The Secretary of State for Wales will be publishing a Green Paper for the teaching profession in Wales, but endorses the core principles covering teachers' pay and career structures. The Government will bring forward its proposals for education in Scotland in a White Paper in January 1999.

166 We intend to consult widely and actively on our proposals which, we recognise, have far-reaching implications for all those who work in the education service and for all who have an interest in its success. We want the consultation exercise to be one of the most thorough mounted in education. We want our proposals to be widely discussed. We will also look at the implications for other parts of the education service outside schools, including further education and sixth form colleges.

167 We set out at the start of this Paper our objectives:

- to develop an education system which achieves consistently high standards, has high expectations of all children whatever their circumstances, seeks constant improvement and takes change in its stride;
- to recognise the key role of teachers in raising standards;
- to ensure we have excellent leadership in every school;
- to exploit the opportunities for new approaches to teaching and learning which additional staff and investment in Information and Communication Technology make possible;
- to provide rewards for success and incentives for excellence;
- to create a culture in which all staff in the education service benefit from good quality training and development throughout their careers so that they can adopt proven best practice and innovative ideas and manage constant change;
- to attract a sufficient supply of good teachers and a greater share of the able and talented; and
- to improve the esteem in which the teaching profession holds itself and is held by the community.

Teachers and their unions

168 Teachers, support staff and their trade unions will clearly have a direct interest in our proposals. We will consult with them about the principles of a new pay and reward structure, and will particularly value their views on the practical implementation issues. We will also be sending copies of a summary of the Green Paper to all school staff.

Parents

169 Parents will have a very substantial interest. The underlying aim of all the proposals – to help the recruitment and retention of good teachers, to improve skills, morale and motivation – is to transform the standard and quality of education for all our children. Children's chances in life are directly and immediately affected by the quality of their teachers.

Local Education Authorities

170 Local Education Authorities have a particular interest in the Green Paper as national employers as well as in the light of their wider responsibilities for school standards. We hope they will share our vision for an education service second to none and help us create a modern, flexible and efficient public service which responds to the needs and wishes of local communities. We hope Diocesan Authorities will also share our aims.

171 Our proposals aim to strengthen the teaching profession and the leadership of schools in ways which will improve standards and help Local Education Authorities implement their own Education Development Plans. Intervention by Local Education Authorities in schools should be in inverse proportion to success. Within that overall framework authorities have an important role to play in taking the proposals forward. In particular we will look to them:

- to encourage the spread of good ideas through their own support work;

- to bring their advisory services up to date – in particular as regards personnel advice – in the light of the proposals in this Green Paper;

- to make good use of teachers' expertise, as many already do, through temporary secondments as well as by recruiting teachers into their own advisory services;

- to provide high quality support for training teachers, teaching assistants, school support staff and schools governors in implementing the proposals in this Green Paper;

- to facilitate headteacher appraisal and to support performance pay for heads by providing comparative information on school achievements and salary levels; and

- to encourage schools to work together in partnership, for example, through their ICT networks or through the Small School Support Fund.

School governors

172 All school governors will have a keen interest in our proposals whatever the type of school. School governing bodies are responsible for the overall conduct of their school. They have a specific duty to do so with a view to promoting high standards of educational achievement. They are employers in practice, even where the formal contract is with the Local Education Authority. They are also responsible for the use of schools' devolved budgets – within which staffing is easily the largest part.

173 Our proposals aim to help governing bodies by providing the tools and funds for better trained, managed and motivated school staff who will be in a position to teach all pupils to their full potential. We will look to governing bodies to play their part in implementing the new arrangements, in particular by updating and operating their salary policies in the light of the new pay system. We will also expect governing bodies to ensure proper appraisal of headteachers whose professional judgement will be so important in making the new system work.

174 We will support governing bodies by being very clear about how the new systems should work; by offering model policies; by providing training for heads in the new system; by offering outside help with processes such as headteacher appraisal where national consistency is essential. We will provide funding to help governors for these purposes.

Chapter 6: Conclusion

Consultation process

175 The consultation process starts with the publication of this document, which is being sent to all schools and to all interested organisations. We would welcome comments on all aspects of the Green Paper from all of those with an interest, in particular on:

Vision

- focus on higher status, better prospects, a rewarding career structure, less bureaucracy, and more freedom to focus on teaching in return for a new professionalism, greater individual accountability, more flexibility and higher standards; and

Timetable

176 The proposals in this Paper go across a wide range of areas and different aspects will go ahead in parallel. We envisage that the overall timetable should be:

Activity	1998 Dec	1999 Jan Mar Jun Sep	2000 Jan Sep	2001 Jan Sep	2002 Jan Sep
Green Paper consultation including conferences	██████				
Recommendations received from School Teachers Review Body (STRB) for the following year		▪	▪	▪	▪
Implementation of main Green Paper proposals on pay and structure			███	████████	████████
Appraisal arrangements in force			██████	████████	████████
School Performance Award Scheme			███	████████	████████
Improvements in initial teacher training			██████	████████	████████
Fast-track Consultation		▪			
Fast-track Implementation			PILOT ███	████████	████████
New programmes for career and professional development			███	████████	████████
National College for School Leadership Consultation		▪			
National College for School Leadership Implementation				████████	████████
More classroom assistants			███	████████	████████

- the proposed new structure for the teaching profession.

Leadership
- broadening the leadership group with more pay and greater use of fixed term contracts for tough headship jobs and effective performance-related pay; and
- a prestigious National College for School Leadership and a new national training framework for headship.

Performance management
- appraisal of teachers' performance management as the basis for professional judgements on pay and career development;
- a performance threshold giving access to higher pay for teachers with a consistently strong performance; and
- a School Performance Award Scheme to reward achievement by whole schools.

Training
- more flexibility and more rigour in initial teacher training;
- systematic career and professional development; and
- a national fast-track scheme to help talented trainees and teachers advance rapidly in the profession.

Better support
- more effective use of, and better training for, teaching assistants and other support staff; and
- a Small School Support Fund to help pilot innovative approaches to schools sharing resources and working closely together where that will help raise educational standards.

177 We want the fullest possible dialogue about the future shape of the profession. A series of seven regional conferences will be launched in January 1999 with other consultation events to present the proposals at local level. A presentation pack will be available on request to schools or organisations which want to arrange their own discussions. We hope that many schools and Local Education Authorities will want to do so.

Responses to consultation

178 We welcome your views on the contents of this Green Paper. A response form is available for your comments and summary, Braille and audio versions of this publication are available free of charge by ringing 0845 601 2518 (local rate). Copies of the Green Paper, summary version and response form are also available on the DfEE website at **www.dfee.gov.uk**
You are invited to return your response form by email to **teachers@numbers.co.uk** or by post to:

DfEE Teachers
FREEPOST
13th Floor, Crown House,
Linton Road, Barking,
Essex IG11 8BR

179 Under the Code of Practice on Open Government, any responses will be made available to the public on request, unless respondents indicate that they wish their response to remain confidential. The consultation period runs until **31 March 1999**.

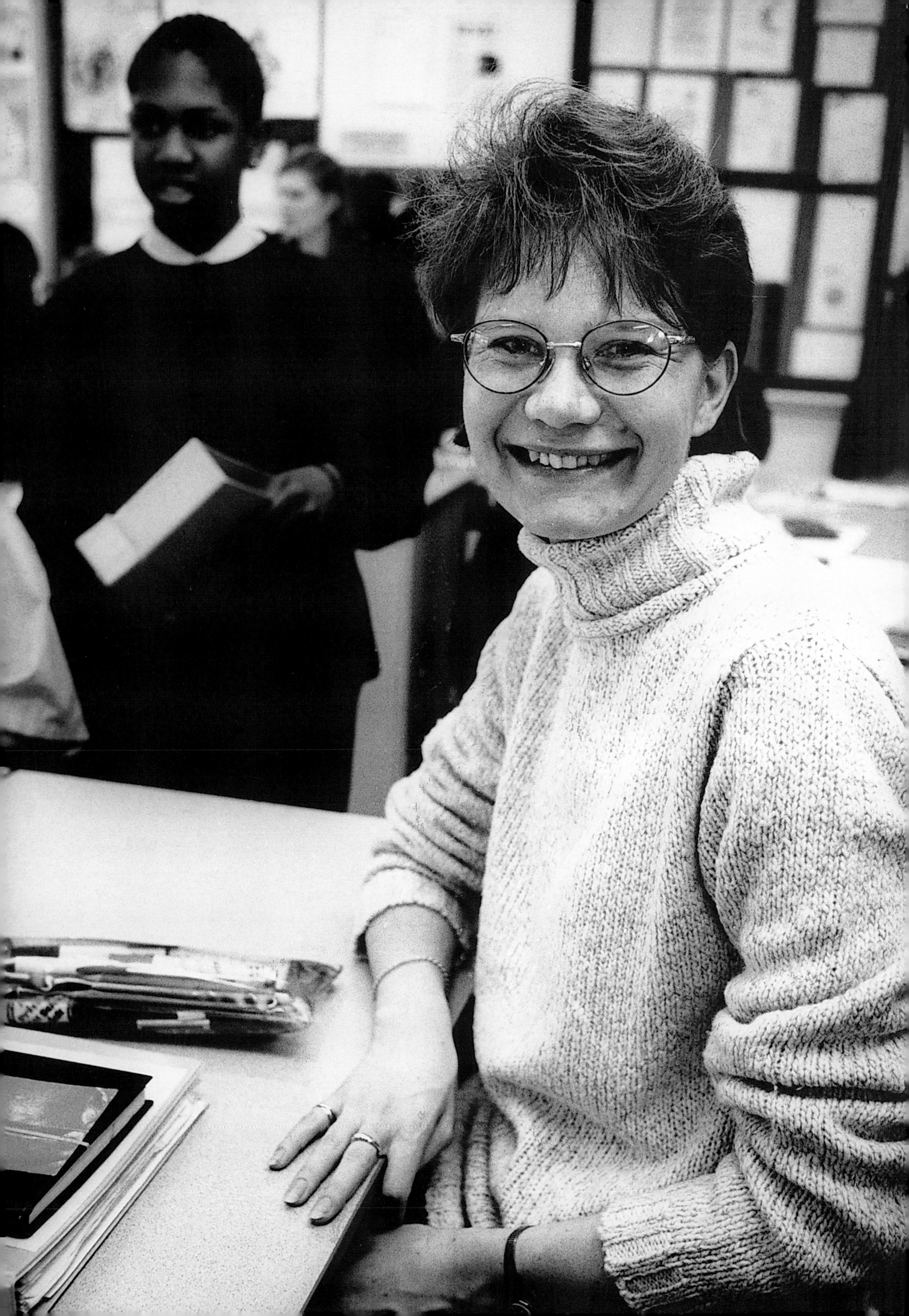

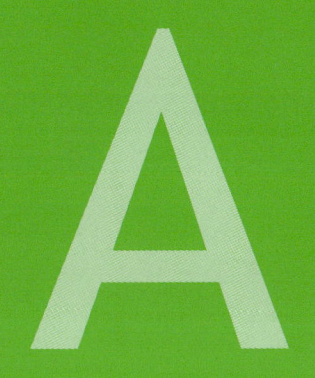

Annex:
Teacher recruitment measures of October 1998

Recruitment measures

On 27 October 1998, the Government announced a £130 million package of measures designed to boost teacher recruitment in the short term. These measures are in addition to the already strong programme of action being taken forward by the Teacher Training Agency (TTA). The major new Government initiatives are:

First: From September 1999 a new £5,000 financial incentive for all those graduates training and going on to teach the key shortage subjects of maths and science will be introduced. This will comprise a £2,500 training incentive for all those entering a postgraduate course in maths or science from next September followed by a further £2,500 payment when those trainees enter teaching. These payments are in addition to the existing special student support measures already introduced for teacher training: the full waiver of the tuition fee for **all** PGCE students and the £10m hardship fund for those in secondary shortage subjects.

Second: A new scheme will be introduced to provide 600 new maths and science teachers. 600 of the 7,000 people who have already told the TTA they would like to train on-the-job as teachers will be matched to maths and science vacancies arising in schools. £2,000 will be put into schools who take these trainees in addition to the £4,000 they would receive under existing arrangements and the TTA will draw up new off-the-shelf training packages to make the school's job easier. The first new trainees should be placed from April 1999.

Third: A new network of advisers at regional level will co-ordinate and energise local recruitment activities in areas of the country with particular shortages. Their mission will be to galvanise 'marketing' of the profession locally; to target potential returners to the profession and match them to refresher courses and jobs; to boost opportunities for on the job training, taking advantage of our new scheme; to smooth the way for good overseas teachers who wish to work in the UK; and to publicise local schemes to help teachers with childcare and housing. Some of these people will be funded directly by DfEE and will be based with Local Education Authorities, others will be based with HE training providers and will be supported by the TTA.

Fourth: The Employment Service will continue to encourage unemployed people with the right experience and qualifications to train or return to teaching. This could be particularly valuable in bringing people from industry into teaching technology.

Fifth: The Government is launching a drive to encourage returners to teaching. Because the pensions disincentive which previously discouraged returners has been removed, a retired teacher will now be able to return to teaching on a full-time basis for at least six months of the year or work half-time (or frequently more) throughout the year without losing any of their retirement pension. Regional advisers will also target and support returners locally.